C000003055

CADDIE IN THE GOLDEN AGE

Also by Jim Gregson

FOR SALE WITH CORPSE

BRING FORTH YOUR DEAD

FOX IN THE FOREST

MURDER AT THE NINETEENTH

DEAD ON COURSE

STRANGLEHOLD

GOLF RULES OK

TAKE UP GOLF

CADDIE
IN THE
GOLDEN AGE

My Years with WALTER HAGEN and HENRY COTTON

Ernest Hargreaves with Jim Gregson

PARTRIDGE PRESS

LONDON · NEW YORK · TORONTO · SYDNEY · AUCKLAND

TRANSWORLD PUBLISHERS LTD
61–63 Uxbridge Road, London W5 5SA

TRANSWORLD PUBLISHERS (AUSTRALIA) PTY LTD
15–25 Helles Avenue, Moorebank, NSW 2170

TRANSWORLD PUBLISHERS (NZ) LTD
3 William Pickering Drive, Albany, Auckland

Published 1993 by Partridge Press
a division of Transworld Publishers Ltd
Copyright © Jim Gregson

The right of Ernest Hargreaves and Jim Gregson to be identified
as authors of this work has been asserted in accordance
with sections 77 and 78 of the Copyright Designs and
Patents Act 1988.

A catalogue record for this book is available from the British Library.
ISBN 185225 1948

This book is sold subject to the Standard Conditions of Sale of Net Books and
not be re-sold in the UK below the net price fixed by the publishers for the
book.

All rights reserved. No part of this publication may
be reproduced, stored in a retrieval system, or
transmitted in any form or by any means,
electronic, mechanical, photocopying, recording,
or otherwise, without the prior permission of
the publishers.

Typeset in 11/14pt Times by
County Typesetters, Margate, Kent.

Printed in Great Britain by
Biddles Ltd, Guildford and King's Lynn.

To Ivy Hargreaves and Rose Gregson.
Two spouses who have coped sympathetically
over the years with the schoolboys who
lurk in the hearts of all golfers.

CONTENTS

CHAPTER ONE

A GOLFING PROLOGUE

I WAS BORN EARLY IN 1913 AT HOLBECK, IN LEEDS. WHEN I was nine months old, the family moved to Allwoodley. I was not consulted over the decision, but it was a move which was to shape my later life.

My father knew me but briefly, and I remember him not at all. He died, like so many other young men of his era, in the Great War, the one that was supposed to end all wars. He was killed in Palestine in September 1914, when I was not yet two. He was defending it from the Jews, among others: the people who were given the region in 1948, after I in turn had fought a war. But I have long since ceased to be astonished by the ironies of war.

The death of my father left my mother with the task of bringing up a family of three. It was a grievous blow, but not quite the financial disaster which death brought to many of those bereaved in that awful conflict. My father had been a regular soldier with a commission, a major in the Green Howards. The compensation for death had been fixed in an era when military deaths were counted in hundreds, not hundreds of thousands, and a grateful nation could afford to be generous to the families of its fallen. Mother got a pension of four pounds a week. At a time when a manual labourer's wage was still not much more than a pound, this was a generous sum.

I had two older sisters, but I was now the only male in the household. Because I was the youngest and the only boy, I was, no doubt, a little spoiled; my sisters tell me so, but I cannot remember it.

As far as material goods went, we were never in debt, but there was not much opportunity to indulge anyone. My mother thought herself lucky to have a job. She was one of only seven workers, all of them women, in the workshops of Burton's, bespoke tailors to the gentry – what was later to become Montague Burton's, with branches throughout Britain and much of what was then the Empire.

But that was far in the future. In 1914 my mother, left with three young children, was grateful to have work. She was a highly competent woman, who would eventually be in charge of a workshed employing two hundred people. But in 1914 she thought of herself merely as lucky to have the chance to support her children: this was still essentially the Edwardian world, when for the working classes, the workhouse and the orphanage were parts of every urban landscape, visual reminders of the need for industry and thrift.

Her only son, growing up without a father to control him, must have been a constant worry to her, for he got into all the usual scrapes a healthy young lad contrives for himself. Being a sound Yorkshireman in the making, he

2

buckled on his clogs and went out to play football all winter and cricket all summer.

In 1924 he got his scholarship to Leeds Grammar School, and his mother breathed a sigh of relief for the future. The postwar boom had burst by then, and hard times were at hand, but a grammar school education should surely guarantee the lad and his family an income of some sort.

Mrs Hargreaves clung to that idea, even when her son proved no great scholar. And in a way her hopes were justified, though it was not in the way she would have chosen. In 1925 some of the lad's peer group at school told him there was easy money to be made, at weekends, carrying bags of golfing sticks for the affluent rich of the city at Moortown Golf Club. He lived within half a mile of the course: this was an earning opportunity which had to be investigated.

The snag was that I was not content merely to lug the bags around on my diminutive shoulders and take my shilling, as others were. I performed my functions adequately enough. I learned quickly where to stand; how to keep quiet and still; how to keep my young eyes sternly on that tiny round ball as it rolled into the distant rough; how to keep a deadpan Christian face through my employers' welters of obscenities and profanities.

But I also became fascinated by this weird and ancient game. It surely could not be as difficult as these middle-aged and portly men made it appear. After all, one approached a dead ball, in one's own time, with no opponent to deliver an unplayable ball or make a crushing tackle. It had to be easy.

One night I experimented behind the caddies' shed when no-one was about. A boy whose father was a player

3

had been given an old club: we found four balls in the deep rough which lined the course and set out to hit them in the dusk.

It was not easy, after all.

The discovery only made me more interested in the game. I began to see that some of the players for whom I caddied hit the ball much better and more accurately than others. Some of them could even get out of sand, without the hard swearing which I had originally thought was part of the ritual of bunkers. I began to read about the great players. When I thought no-one was looking I even tried setting my hands on the grips of the clubs I carried in the mystical manner advocated by the great Harry Vardon.

In 1926, at the age of thirteen, I attended my first Open. I did not miss another for fifty-two years. My first one saw twenty-four-year-old Bobby Jones win at Lytham; my final one as a worker saw perhaps the greatest last-day duel of all, between Jack Nicklaus and Tom Watson, at Turnberry in 1977. I have made intermittent pilgrimages to Opens since then, but the great crowds and the fact that the spectators are kept so far away from the players have driven me to television.

I was lucky in that first Open at Lytham. Jones, coming there from what most people said was the most perfect round ever played, in the qualifying competition at Sunningdale, won in the lowest four-round total ever recorded. He played golf such as I had never seen before. Four Americans filled the first four places, and Walter Hagen, the only golfer whom even non-golfers had heard about, came third.

Hagen had an opening 68, the first round I had ever seen anywhere which broke 70. Years later I realized that he had smiled at the whole great bank of spectators around the eighteenth as he left the green; at the time I thought his smile was for the one small boy who was applauding him so hard. He had a new fan to add to the millions who already followed him.

I was there again for the Open of 1927 at St Andrews. There was a scoreboard beside the eighteenth green which showed us who was leading as the scores came in – a big improvement on the single small sheet pinned to a board at which we had peered in the previous years.

It was the first time I had seen the famous old course, and Jones scored an opening 68, a record score, which I almost thought had been specially designed for me by the Almighty. I cheered as loudly as anyone when Jones won the championship by a clear six shots from Aubrey Boomer. A twenty-year-old Englishman called T. H. Cotton came ninth, losing eight shots against Jones on the last day.

In 1928 I went down south for the first time in my life, to Sandwich, where I walked miles before I heard a northern accent. But I was fifteen now, old enough to be a man; the state thought so, for it let people leave school at fourteen and go to work, though my mother had made me stay on at school. My long journey was well worth the while. My hero, Walter Hagen, won by two shots from Gene Sarazen, and I saw it all.

On the train home, I found a copy of a golfing magazine; in those far-off days, they rushed out a special edition to cover the Open. I read it eagerly, reliving every shot of Hagen's triumph. In a small paragraph on the back page, I read that it was thought that the Ryder Cup, the newly established contest between Britain and America, would be played in Britain in 1929, at Moortown Golf

Club in Leeds. Walter Hagen was expected to select and captain the American team.

Moortown! The club where I carried bags for members; where I knew every inch of the course! My mind filled with wild ideas. I think I fell asleep as the train rocked rapidly northwards. I know I left the magazine behind in the confusion of gathering my belongings at Leeds.

But I had formed a resolution which would shape the rest of my life.

CHAPTER TWO

A DREAM SURPASSED
BY REALITY

ON 23 MAY 1929, THE AMERICAN RYDER CUP TEAM LEFT
the Queen's Hotel in Leeds and boarded their taxis for
the short journey to Moortown Golf Club.

Long before they did so, I had arrived at the club on
foot, determined to be in good time for what I was
convinced was to be the greatest week of my golfing life.
Young dreams like that are there to be shattered; that is
one of the harsh experiences of life. This dream was the
one in a million which life chose to surpass.

I wore the spotless uniform of Leeds Grammar School,
where I was still a reluctant and only fitfully industrious
pupil. At school, I derided the uniform to my fellow-
pupils; now I saw it as a mantle of respectability. It was
freshly sponged and pressed; I left off only the cap, since
that would have made me a boy, where a man was clearly
required.

There were many men hoping to caddy that week, for
in the midst of a depression affluent Americans suggested

rich pickings. With a very few exceptions, the men who hoped to serve them were a villainous-looking crew. It was almost as if they took it as a matter of honour to look as much as possible like the famous *Punch* cartoons of depraved caddies. I remember them as uniformly scruffy in dress, wearing ill-fitting jackets and coats and a variety of dubious neckwear and moth-ravaged headgear.

Their dress could be excused at a time when many were going hungry and most families had little to spare for clothes, but they carried as a group an air of debauch. At that time in the morning, almost all of them were probably sober, but many showed plainly the results of the previous night's imbibing. Only a minority were freshly shaved, and if cleanliness is really next to godliness they were a devilish crew indeed.

I stood a little way from them in my well-pressed uniform, and I doubt whether they realized that I purposed to be one of their number. That was probably just as well for me.

They surrounded the taxis as they arrived in succession, bringing the American golfers from their hotel. There was excitement and satisfaction for a few as they managed to secure themselves bags for the day. Farrell and Turnesa, Diegel and Golden, American giants who had dominated the first Ryder Cup triumph in 1927, all arrived and were applauded by spectators. I hung back, even when young Gene Sarazen, who seemed scarcely taller than me, climbed laughing and friendly from his cab. I felt like an angler who will cast only for the biggest fish of all.

I had been determined from the start to wait for Walter Hagen, the legendary 'Haig', the man who had established the professional golfer as a glamorous sportsman and ensured that golf was now given extensive coverage in even the popular papers. I might even speak to him. At the worst, I would see the great man at close quarters. At the best . . .

Some time after the rest of the American team had arrived, there was still no sign of Hagen. Perhaps his sense of drama was already at work, preparing an effective entry. I wondered if he would arrive, as we were told he often did, in a Rolls-Royce, making a point to those who looked down their well-bred noses at professional golfers.

He did not. He came in a taxi like the rest. Hagen was captain of the American team, as he was of every one of the first six American Ryder Cup teams. As a member of a team, he chose not to distinguish himself from the other members. When he was playing as an individual, things would be different. Hagen, as I was shortly to learn, had a sense of what was owed to his fellow-professionals as well as his own undoubted sense of style.

When Hagen's cab finally arrived, the Moortown dignitaries moved forward to welcome him. Immediately behind them the caddies waited eagerly to offer their services, for Hagen's generosity towards his golfing acolytes was already a legend. On the other side of the taxi from the great man stood the largest bag of golf clubs I had ever seen.

I acted purely on impulse, and it was an impulse which was to shape the rest of my life. Before I knew quite what was happening or what I proposed to do, I was on the other side of the taxi, calmly removing that bag of clubs, which seemed almost as large as I was myself. I said, as nonchalantly as I could, 'I'll just take these inside for you, sir.'

Then I turned and marched into the Moortown

9

clubhouse I knew so well, expecting at every moment to be recalled by an angry voice asking what the hell I thought I was doing. No such reprimand came, and two minutes later, I found myself standing respectfully beside the captain of the American Ryder Cup team as he exchanged jovial greetings with two luminaries of the Moortown club, Louis Kerby and Lawson Brown.

I did not dare finger any of the actual clubs with which this wizard wrought his magic. But I stood with my right hand placed diffidently on the edge of the big bag, trying to look as though I was mounting guard over it, as though I did this kind of thing every day and confidently expected to be retained by Walter Hagen.

When I heard him say suddenly to Mr Kerby, 'And what kind of a youngster have we got here, then?' it was the first indication that I had had that Hagen had noticed me. Even then it was a moment before I dared to think he was talking about me.

Mr Kerby did not let me down. My diligent politeness to the members of Moortown was rewarded a hundred-fold in his reply: 'Walter, he's a good lad. You can rely on him to look after you!'

I blushed as I looked for the first time into the great man's face, hoping above hope that he would take on my well-scrubbed innocence, willing him to disregard the wealth of tournament-caddying experience which waited noisily outside. I saw a round, amiable face, dominated by shrewd eyes, twinkling with pleasure. It had not many lines, yet it looked to my schoolboy eyes quite old (much later I found that 'the Haig' was at this time thirty-six).

The mobile lips relaxed into the grin I was to get to know so well in the months which followed. 'Looks like you just got yourself a job, Sonny!' he said.

10

* * *

I am sure that Mr Kerby thought Hagen was going to use me just for the first of the practice days, of which there were to be three. I dared to hope for no more than that myself, even as I set out down Moortown's first hole on a bright, cool May morning, pinching myself to confirm that it was really me walking self-importantly behind the world's most famous golfer, struggling to keep my heels clear of the gallery that was already gathering about him.

Gradually during the day it emerged that Hagen would keep me on for the rest of his practice if I was satisfactory, that I might even be beside him for the Ryder Cup itself, if my strength and my behaviour held out.

The strength aspect concerned me not a little, as the adrenalin consequent on my appointment began at last to seep away. The huge bag was made of leather, the handsomest but not the lightest of materials. When I tested things at the end of the day, I found that even when empty it was heavy. When I look at the bags supported by today's tournament caddies, Hagen's bag looks quite modest, but it was bigger than anything I had carried for the members at Moortown. And remember, I was a sixteen-year-old who was small for my age!

Moreover, the bag contained no fewer than sixteen clubs; for another nine years or so, there would be no restrictions on the number of clubs a golfer might carry. All of them had hickory shafts, for steel shafts were not made legal by the Royal and Ancient until 1930. Several of the Americans had to switch from the steel shafts they had been allowed to use in the United States to hickory for the Ryder Cup contest.

The most notable was Horton Smith, the brilliant new prodigy of American golf, who had won all but one of the

11

open tournaments in America he had played in during the first few months of 1929. He was only twenty and the first player to use steel shafts throughout his professional career. He struggled to adapt to hickory over the practice days – it was a strange sight for me, who had never seen steel shafts – and Hagen did not pick him for the foursomes. But he was charming and uncomplaining, and such a fine golfer that he managed to beat Fred Robson four and two in the singles with the hickory shafts he had had to borrow for the contest.

I was so delighted to be carrying for Walter Hagen, so concerned not to do anything which would lose me the precious commission I had acquired, that I cannot remember a lot of detail from the practice days. It was all new to me, and it passed in a colourful blur of continuous excitement.

The Americans were famous golfers, Horton Smith being the only newcomer to the team which had thrashed Great Britain in the initial contest in America two years previously (the team did not become 'Great Britain and Ireland' until 1973). And, of course, there was a much greater thrill then in seeing these great names on the course than there would be today, since there was no television to beam pictures around the world, and the silent cinema newsreels did not yet think golf worthy of their attention. Even on the practice days, there were crowds of spectators, not least because admission was free and we Yorkshire folk have never been people to pass up a bargain!

The Americans behaved impeccably. The atmosphere was almost like a public school outing, though many of the players had come up the hard way, starting as caddies and moving on to the circuit when they had honed their skills and their confidence in money matches. They were gracious and friendly with the crowds, willing to discuss the clubs they were taking and what they were attempting to do with the ball when they struck it. At the end of the contest, one of them actually gave away his shoes to a member of the gallery.

Not least among them was the great man himself. Like most of the others, Hagen selected his club and hit the ball without fuss and preliminaries. He then strolled purposefully but unhurriedly after it. With my great burden and my diminutive steps, I was often driven to a clumsy trot beneath the bag to keep up with him. What saved me was his habit of conversing with the spectators. He kept them continually amused with his comments on his efforts, which were usually derogatory.

And if he saw an interesting person in the crowd he would stop for conversation, about golf or anything else that occurred to his busy, jackdaw mind. 'Interesting' more often than not meant a pretty girl. He ran a practised eye over the ranks of his supporters and rarely missed a chance to exchange words with the female element among them. I suppose many Americans in our more serious age would accord him the 'chauvinist' label they bestow so easily, but most of the ladies he spoke to were both charmed and flattered by his attention, and nothing improper was ever suggested. Many of them were invited back to the Queen's Hotel in the evenings, where Hagen and his team held their social court until after midnight.

With the callow judgement of youth, I was not very impressed by the Hagen I saw on those practice days. If this was the greatest golfer in the world, he did not obey most of the canons I had read about and seen my British

13

heroes implement. He swayed on every shot, and he got himself into some spots on the course which even the good amateurs I had watched at Moortown would not have found. It was true that he often seemed to end up on or very near the green when I had not expected him to – but a great golfer should surely be more impressive than this.

It was not until later that I understood how little he cared for practice. On the second hole we played, he put his second shot into a difficult place to the right of the green, surveyed it for a moment, and said, 'Just pick that one up, Sonny.' He strolled off to the next tee and the girl beside it he had decided was more worthy of his attention. Several times more he did not bother to play out a hole where he had made a mistake. But when I reviewed the practice days as I lay in bed at home, I realized that at one time or another he had putted out on every green at least once, and decided on each tee where he wished to place his drive.

In other words, his casual attitude was both genuine and to some extent a pose. He was perfectly relaxed, as much at ease with himself and those around him as he appeared to be. Yet he was shrewd and observant the while, with a golfing brain that knew what it was looking for and stored the information without obvious effort. The more I saw of him in that momentous year of 1929, the more impressed I was by this combination of playboy and professional.

On the day before the contest, as excitement mounted and the Leeds hotels filled with spectators coming to watch the first Ryder Cup match in Britain, the contest was threatened by an event peculiarly British. Although we had practised in the morning – you will note that I now

14

considered myself experienced enough to use the traditional caddie's 'we', except where my man made a mistake, when I reverted immediatly to 'he' – Hagen had played no more than half-a-dozen holes before declaring himself ready for the contest and repairing to more amenable surroundings indoors, away from the bitter wind. I had cleaned every speck of dirt from his two-tone golf shoes and put the shoe-trees in them as soon as he came off the course – already I had learned the routine of my part in his impeccable appearance on the course. Then I made sure that each of the clubs was wiped and polished ready for action on the morrow: I had a shrewd suspicion we should not be practising again in the afternoon.

In the event, no-one did. On the afternoon of 25 May, one and a half inches of snow fell on the course at Moortown. Golfers and members stared bleakly through plate glass at the whitening course; newspaper photographers delightedly climbed as high as they could to get pictures of Arctic wastes which had been impeccable fairways an hour or two earlier. People said glumly that the match would have to be postponed.

And the youngest caddie engaged for the contest prayed hard and unashamedly through the evening that all might yet be well.

And it was. This was the end of May, after all, and when I arrived at the course at seven o'clock next morning there was no sign of snow. The greens, already swished clear of moisture by the staff, were in perfect condition.

The American team were in immaculate pale-blue cashmere sweaters with roll necks, which were considered by some diehards to be daringly casual; it was an era when

15

most people still played in collars and ties, and jackets had not long been discarded. With the plus-fours which were then the routine male golfing garment and highly polished shoes, they looked very smart in what was, in effect, a team uniform. The British were more individual and less debonair, with a variety of colours and conditions among the woollens being sported on that brisk May morning.

Hagen wore the two-tone golfing shoes which were already one of his trade marks. The only British player who gave the same attention to his dress was twenty-two-year-old Henry Cotton, who had been befriended by the Haig when he went to America in the winter of 1928–9 to further the learning of his trade and was already beginning to favour the monogrammed silk shirts and gold cuff-links of his mentor.

So it was no surprise to find Cotton wearing two-tone brown-and-white 'Cotton Oxford' shoes, which would later become his trade mark. In commercial matters, as in other things, Henry was a quick learner and hardly ever repeated a mistake!

All matches then were over thirty-six holes, this being considered the minimum distance for a fair match. Play on the first day consisted of four foursome matches. With his usual sense of drama, Walter Hagen, who was playing with Johnny Golden, was in the last of these matches. I found that they were to play Ernest Whitcombe, my big-hitting boyhood hero, and young Henry Cotton, the golden boy of British golf and my own new idol.

It was the match everyone wanted to see, and though each of the three matches ahead of us had its following, more and more of the spectators drifted back to get a glimpse of ours: as well as having the most glamorous participants, it had golf of breathtaking quality and was tightly contested throughout the day.

Beside the first tee, Hagen introduced me to the rest of the golfers and anyone else who cared to listen. 'This is my boy caddie, Sonny,' he said, and tapped me lightly on the head. It was the way he introduced me to people throughout the summer. He never called me anything but 'Sonny', just as for forty years Cotton was never to call me anything but 'Hargreaves'. Each of them was courteous and considerate of my needs; each of them behaved throughout our association as a gentleman.

Hagen said to me quietly as he waited his turn to tee up, 'Let's have a look at our book then, Sonny.' I produced the notebook on which I had worked with loving care over the previous three evenings. In my meticulous schoolboy hand I had drawn a picture of each hole, with details such as bunkers and distances from prominent landmarks beside each fairway. Such aids were then frowned upon; it is only in the last generation that the Royal and Ancient has bowed to the inevitable and allowed the publication of 'course guides', nowadays usually available to the visitor in the pro's shop.

Hagen always demanded such detail of the course from his caddie, and consulted the notebook on almost every hole. I think he was the first of the great professionals to do this, although others quickly followed. It is evidence again of the very serious golfing brain Hagen concealed beneath his social panache.

Foursomes was then played as it ought to be, as the fastest of all golfing games. There were over five thousand spectators at Moortown (that is the official figure, though the ten thousand Cotton quotes in one of his books may be nearer the mark, for the numbers grew on

17

the second day as a British success seemed possible), but there were no stewards to marshal them or ropes to confine them to particular areas. The biggest crowds seemed to gather round our match, yet we completed the morning round in two hours and forty-three minutes, with Ernest Whitcombe thinking that it had really been rather tardy because we had several times to wait for the crowds to clear!

My man Hagen played well enough, but he seemed almost disappointed when his partner regularly hit the fairways. It was only on the couple of occasions when he found himself in awkward places that he was able to set the spectators gasping with the brilliance and imagination of his recovery shots. 'When I'm playing my own drives, I get plenty of practice from places like this!' he explained modestly, when a spectator complimented him on a high fade with a mashie (5-iron) to the sixteenth.

Even during the match, he was as relaxed as ever, prepared to converse with spectators about the state of the stock market or the British general election, due four days later, as easily as about the golf. I was quite grateful for such respites, having the thick topcoat my mother had insisted I should wear over my arm, as well as the big bag with its stuffed pockets and sixteen clubs to contend with. As the sun rose higher and the temperature climbed, I sweated along beside my immaculate employer in my jacket and tie, forcing my small legs to make good speed.

By the halfway stage at lunch-time, there was not much in three of the matches; but in the fourth Diegel and Espinosa had a good lead for the Americans against Aubrey Boomer and George Duncan.

They consolidated this in the afternoon, running out winners by seven and five. In the first match out, Farrell

18

and Turnesa halved an exciting struggle with Charles Whitcombe (Ernest's brother) and Archie Compston. The British pair appeared to have the match won when Joe Turnesa hooked his second to the seventeenth behind the refreshment marquee which had been erected beside the clubhouse. There was some discussion about whether there should be a free drop – I have no doubt that a modern professional would have waited for a decision, since the marquee was obviously not a normal part of the course.

Instead, Johnny Farrell, whose turn it was to play, grinned at someone in the crowd who asked him to 'Show us a good niblick shot, Johnny!' He then proceeded to do just that, flicking the ball from a difficult lie high into the air and over the tent to the invisible green. It landed softly and rolled up to within two feet of the hole. The tumultuous roar of the crowd told Farrell how perfectly he had responded to his customer's suggestion. A few minutes later, the match was halved on the thirty-sixth.

In the third match, immediately ahead of ours, Abe Mitchell and Fred Robson held their nerve over the last few holes to ensure a British victory by two and one. Things were all square, with one match to each side and one halved. There were no boards to relay the state of matches, but the news ran quickly back down the course. How the whole match stood at the end of the first day would depend on our match.

Cotton and Ernest Whitcombe were one down for most of the afternoon. Time after time, they seemed to me to play a hole better than the opposition, but time after time the Americans held on. As the excitement mounted, it did not seem possible to my agitated young mind that a man could be as calm in that situation as Hagen was. Several times he listened to friendly suggestions from the increasingly animated crowd as to the shot he should play. I am sure he was perfectly clear in his own mind about what he proposed to do and with which club, but he loved communicating with people and could not bear to play in a glum silence.

And how he played! With a regularity depressing to his opponents, he would put the ball on to, or near, the green from a difficult position. Most of the crucial putts seemed to fall to him after his partner had missed one or two early in the afternoon. The more the tension grew, the more securely he holed out. As a raw young lad, who had thought golf was all about swinging the club gracefully, I began to appreciate for the first time how big a part temperament played in the top reaches of this fascinating game.

The Americans held on to halves when they might have lost at the sixteenth and seventeenth, and came to the last hole still one up. The British could still halve the match and leave the whole Ryder Cup contest poised level overnight. It felt, on the crowded eighteenth tee, as if the whole of Leeds was willing them to do so.

The Britons were almost on in two after a good drive. Hagen, as though determined to have drama to the last, faded his second just too much and left his partner with a difficult pitch. Golden played it well, but left his captain a seven-footer. The British missed from just outside them, whereupon Hagen walked up to his ball, surveyed it for perhaps two seconds, and knocked it nonchalantly into the hole for a win. I think he almost wished the British putt had gone in, to keep the pressure on him!

Golden and Hagen had won the match two up. The four players came in to prolonged applause for a splendid match, and the Americans led overnight by two and a half to one and a half.

So far in this remarkable five days, I had hardly had a moment for reflection. On the evening in the middle of the match, with the balance tilted towards the Americans, I found myself wondering if I still wanted Great Britain to win.

A week earlier it would have been inconceivable that I should even consider the matter. I had been waiting for the contest to arrive with that impatience possible only for a schoolboy, desperately anxious for a British victory to avenge the 9½–2½ thrashing we had taken in the inaugural contest on the other side of the Atlantic. But a caddie's loyalty is to the man he carries for, and the magnetism of Walter Hagen was reinforced for me by that strong bond.

I decided that I should like Hagen to win his match, but Great Britain to win the whole contest. It was the first of my dreams in that magic week which was not fulfilled, though part of it came true.

George Duncan, the British captain, was an awesome figure to me. Tall and ramrod straight, he was then forty-five, but still without the hint of a grey hair. He was the Open Champion of 1920, and much respected by his fellow-professionals. I would find in the years to come that he was a kind and considerate man: he was the son of a village policeman and one of ten children, so he had seen plenty of the harsher side of life. But on that bright morning of 27 May 1929, he seemed, to a boy almost thirty years his junior, a remote and fearsome presence. He had the air of a man who would not suffer fools gladly, and I was very careful throughout the day not to per-petrate anything foolish.

Duncan called together his team for a pow-wow before the eight thirty-six hole singles matches that would settle the contest. Hagen grinned and refused to hold any such meeting for his team. His attitude was that they were professionals who knew exactly how they should be tackling things. Even at lunch-time, he would confine himself to checking how the matches were going and offering the odd word of encouragement. There could be no greater contrast with the intense, white-faced tautness of his successors as Ryder Cup captains half a century later, but I don't think the efforts of his team on the course were any the less for his relaxed attitude.

There has been speculation ever since 1929 that Hagen or Duncan or both fixed the draw so that they should play each other. In fact, there was no draw in the accepted sense. I saw Hagen write his team up on a blackboard in the clubhouse! Duncan, who was watching, said with a smile, 'Well, I'll play you then, Walter,' and things were arranged as simply as that. The protocol of the exchange of team sheets came later: in those far-off days things were quite informal. I think the two captains arranged to play each other as being the appropriate thing, just as they might have done in a friendly match between two golf clubs.

We were second off, with the biggest gallery of all. I quickly found I had a new problem.

George Duncan was the fastest player I ever saw. Every time I watch Bernhard Langer, Nick Faldo or Curtis Strange, I long to see them for just one round with Duncan, in the hope that a little of that earlier and simpler age might rub off on the moderns.

Duncan walked to his ball, dropped his limbs into his

stance immediately, without even the hint of a shuffle, and hit the ball. If he ever studied the line and the shape of his shot, he had done it before he reached his ball, for there was no pause when he got to it. As for practice swings, he regarded them as totally unnecessary and barely legal – close to practising on the course!

The great James Braid, who knew Duncan well, wrote: 'I cannot make him out. He plays so fast that he looks as if he doesn't care, but I suppose it must be his way. He's the most extraordinary golfer I have ever seen.'

The result of his approach was that I was hard pressed to keep up with the match, for Duncan strode forward as soon as he had played his shot, and the crowd followed hard on his heels, and even harder on mine! I was reduced sometimes to a lumbering run, with fearful backward glances which caused some amusement in the section of the crowd near enough to see my discomfort.

Duncan was accused by many others, as well as Braid, of playing *too* quickly: people pointed to his mixture of good and bad rounds and reasoned that if he had been able to add consistency by taking just a little time to consider his shot, he would have won even more. But George argued that he could not play in any other way, that his temperament simply did not permit him a different tempo. He called his autobiography *Golf at the Gallop*, and there never was a more appropriate title: the memory of how I raced along on that sparkling May morning remains vivid well over sixty years later.

That day, in perhaps the most famous match he ever played, Duncan's method could not be faulted. His golf was quite simply brilliant. I cannot remember him dropping a shot to par – or bogey, as we thought of it then in this country – all day, and he improved upon it several

23

times. He made golf seem a very simple business indeed, and his speed of execution made it look as if he expected it to be so.

Walter Hagen was not exactly ruffled – I never saw that in his demeanour on a golf course, whatever his inner thoughts. But I think the speed, brilliance and simplicity of his opponent's golf had its effect. He hit more bad shots than usual, and for once the quality of his recovery play was not consistent enough to keep him in the match. In effect, the result was settled in the first hour, after which Duncan was six up. Hagen was complimentary about his opponent's play, and humorously deprecating about his own; but he could not disguise from himself or anyone else that he was taking a thrashing.

Duncan completed his morning's work in under two and a half hours, and went to lunch eight up. I crept away, cleaned my sixteen clubs, and tried to keep clear of my employer. My experience with the members of Moortown had taught me that the caddies of unsuccessful golfers could be treated like Roman messengers who brought bad news. We needed to play only ten holes in the afternoon. My man got a few halves, but there was no coming back against Duncan that day: Walter Hagen, the most famous golfer in the world, lost by ten and eight.

It meant that our match was the first one to finish, so that I was able to see the others come in over the last few holes. The crushing nature of Hagen's defeat has tended to obscure the fact that the United States had a victory just as overwhelming in the match behind ours, in which Leo Diegel defeated that glorious striker Abe Mitchell by nine and eight. That left the United States still one match ahead in the overall scoring, but cheers from the crowd around the twelfth green announced almost immediately that Charles Whitcombe had levelled the score, beating Johnny Farrell by eight and six in the first match out.

There was some dispute over whether Aubrey Boomer should in fact have been playing, since he was professional at St Cloud in Paris and the convention then was that only players resident in Britain should be selected (Cotton was to miss out on three Ryder Cups because of the regulation). But that was all forgotten as he came in with a four-and-three win against Turnesa. When we heard that Archie Compston had crushed Gene Sarazen by six and four, hopes were high indeed.

Sarazen, who played nine holes at the head of the field for the Masters at Augusta in 1992, when he had passed ninety, is the only one of the contestants in the 1929 Ryder Cup who is still alive at the time of writing, and I am the only surviving caddie. He was followed throughout the week by an enthusiastic Italian contingent, many of them from among the ice-cream makers of Leeds, and he welcomed them enthusiastically on and off the course.

On the previous day, Horton Smith had sought and been given advice on the use of his unfamiliar hickory shafts from his opponent, the kindly and courteous Fred Robson. Robson was a skilled clubmaker and a highly respected teacher. Young Horton Smith used his lesson to such good effect that he now beat Robson four and two!

The margin of the British lead was thus reduced to a single match, but there were only two of the singles left. If Henry Cotton, the great new hope of British golf, whom everyone said would one day win the Open, could win his match, victory would be Great Britain's, whatever happened in the closely contested final match. Against Al Watrous, Cotton had had a remarkable stroke of luck at the eighteenth in the morning, when he holed out with his niblick from some bushes to win a hole which had seemed irretrievably lost.

He kept his nose in front for most of the afternoon, and he was not going to be caught now. To a mighty cheer, he closed out his match on the fifteenth, to secure a four-and-three victory and ensure that the Ryder Cup would return to Britain.

Poor Ernest Whitcombe, fighting tenaciously to the thirty-sixth hole against Espinosa, came in to the news that his half was not as vital as he had thought for most of the afternoon! Samuel Ryder presented his splendid gold cup, with its effigy of his personal professional, Abe Mitchell, atop the lid, to George Duncan. The crowds gave one last great cheer, and went home happy. The teams fraternized, celebrated the spirit of the contest, and made ready for the journey north to Muirfield and the Open Championship.

And Walter Hagen, who would feature in all the morning papers as the recipient of a most celebrated drubbing, held a conversation with his diminutive caddie behind the Moortown clubhouse. He had maintained his elegant panache upon the course, but he was really very annoyed with himself. 'What rubbish I played today, Sonny,' he said. He looked down at me for comment, but I was not wise enough in the ways of the world to offer him any white lies of consolation. He said, with a grin, 'I wasn't worth caddying for today.'

I managed to get out words to say that I had enjoyed it, hoping I would not sound too mercenary. I had been paid two pounds a day for what I would gladly have done for nothing; my usual rate from members was one shilling for a round.

Hagen said casually, 'Are you going to Muirfield for the Open, Sonny?'

'Oh, yes,' I said, making the decision even as I spoke.

'How about caddying for me then, Sonny?'

I was growing used to having to pinch myself to make sure these things were really happening. Now the most famous golfer in the world, off to defend the greatest title in the world, was asking me to go with him. I said as evenly as I could, 'I'd love to, Mr Hagen.'

'Right then, Sonny. See you there for the practice.' He ambled away to refill his glass and rejoin the party. At the door he turned round and smiled at me. 'I've a feeling I'm going to be lucky at Muirfield.'

CHAPTER THREE

THE OPEN OF 1929

MY FIRST PROBLEM WAS TO GET FROM LEEDS TO MUIRFIELD. It was not quite as simple in 1929 as it would be today. And despite Hagen's generous payment for my Ryder Cup work, I was an impecunious youngster.

At Moortown, I had got to know many of the young journalists who had flooded into Leeds for the Ryder Cup. Some of them were to remain good friends of mine for the next sixty years, whilst each of us in our different ways made a living out of the game we loved. One of them, Maurice Hart, now organized my journey to Muirfield. We got ourselves to Newcastle by charabanc, the cheapest method. From there, he had secured for us two rail tickets to Muirfield at his paper's expense.

Three days before the Open, we were safely installed in the Aberlady Hotel. It was no doubt a modest enough establishment, but it seemed to me palatial. I was living in the lap of luxury, earning my living from golf. More than that: I was about to caddie for the most famous player of his era, friend of presidents and future kings, the one everyone wanted to see play, the one who dominated all the newspaper speculation as the players moved into the town and the excitement grew.

Maurice and I, sixteen-year-old men of the world, tucked into our cooked breakfasts, counted our spare change in private, and tried to pretend that we were old hands at the hotel game.

The entire American Ryder Cup team stayed on for the Open. In addition, twelve other leading Americans made the expensive and time-consuming voyage across the Atlantic by ship, and then the long train journey up to the east coast of Scotland to compete. The exploits of Hagen and Bobby Jones had convinced them that, apart from its revered history, the Open was the nearest thing in existence to a championship of the world.

For those who travelled from afar, the Open was quite an undertaking, for until as late as 1963, when the leading players were exempted, everyone had to play through the qualifying rounds. There was no guarantee that golfers who had travelled great distances, allocating perhaps a month of their time in all and a great deal of money to the enterprise, would even qualify for the Open proper. They had to play through thirty-six holes of the qualifying competition, at Gullane and Muirfield, before they could be sure of appearing in the Championship.

And those young Americans who were finding the new steel shafts to their liking had to switch back to the old hickory for the Open: there was as yet no agreement on such things between the ruling bodies in Britain and America, so the R & A rules applied.

From an initial field of 242 for the qualifying rounds,

ninety-five professionals and fourteen amateurs came through to contest the Open. It was generally agreed in the newspaper previews that this was the strongest field ever to assemble for the event, despite the absence of Bobby Jones. The new Ryder Cup event had ensured that the cream of American golf was here; the strength of the field was highly impressive.

Because of this, even the bookies were giving generous odds on some well-known players. Maurice Hart, in the privacy of our room, deliberated long and hard on where to place his slender resources; even at that tender age, he was the keen gambler he always remained. My mother had warned me against such things, and for once I had the sense to listen to her.

Because of the thrashing he had received from George Duncan in the Ryder Cup, Hagen's chances were played down. Some of the papers dared to wonder whether he was 'over the hill', with his nose put a little out of joint by the clean-cut new American star, Jones, who was in so many ways his antithesis. Being still only sixteen and easily swayed by such things, I was a little doubtful myself. But I reminded myself of the last words the Haig (as his caddie, I now felt I had a proprietorial right to use his universal nickname as we discussed these things) had said to me at Moortown, 'I've a feeling I'm going to be lucky at Muirfield.'

The practice days and the qualifying days were mostly cold and miserable, with a raw wind and rain scudding in intermittently off the Firth of Forth. Most of the British Ryder Cup men were staying at the Grey Walls Hotel. The Ryder Cup Americans and several other prominent players were staying at the Marine Hotel, Gullane, a splendid establishment which was reduced in later years to a fire station! In 1929 it was far too grand to allow anything as humble as a caddie within its portals. I picked up Walter Hagen's bag at the course.

'Hello, Sonny!' he called. He looked up at the low grey skies. 'I'm still confident: we won't waste too much of our time on practice.'

During the practice days, the Haig consistently preferred the comforts and the company of the clubhouse and his hotel (Muirfield did not allow ladies within its hallowed walls, of course) to the privations of the course. It made my job easier, but his movements were unpredictable. I cleaned the clubs assiduously and waited for long hours in the shelter of the caddie shed for my man to emerge.

With time on my hands, I studied the procedures of men who had done this work for years, anxious to pick up any tips I could. But there was no great mystique. We oiled the leather grips, then polished the faces of the irons with emery paper, but carefully left the centre unbuffed: the idea was that the indentations on the faces would not grip if they were made too smooth.

Hagen's laid-back style is legendary, and his reluctance to practise is part of the myth. In fact, he had stored up a bank of practice and experiment in his early years. In an era when most good golfers came to the game only in adolescence, Walter had begun at five. In his autobiography he wrote: 'Golf champions are made, not born. I would be the first to admit that one must have a flair for the game, but only constant practice and concentration on every type of shot will produce the real champion. By the time I was fifteen, I had played more golf and practised more shots than most young golfers of twenty-one today.'

31

Hagen had won the American Open as long ago as 1914. He already had three British Opens when he came to Muirfield in what was to prove the last of his great years. He had the shots in his locker; he did just enough preparation to hone the skills he had developed many years earlier as a young man. And, more than any man I have ever seen, he enjoyed all the trappings of the fame those skills had brought him.

What he did practise was putting. He spent quite a lot of time on the practice putting green, with the explanation to those who watched that it was not far from the shelter of the bar. But he also putted on every green on the course, surveying the borrows from different angles towards what he thought would be the probable pin positions. In those days, it was usual to leave the flags in the same positions for the whole of the championship.

We looked at all the holes, but we never played eighteen holes in practice, or anywhere near that number. The Haig was more interested in the shapes of the holes and the tactics they would need than in rehearsing his shots. He knew that weather can change a course completely in a couple of hours in links golf, that detailed notes about club selection for various shots would be of little or no use.

Meanwhile, I mapped the positions of the various bunkers and meticulously paced out the distances from various landmarks to the greens. From these details I compiled what Hagen would refer to during the Championship as 'our book', just as he had done at Moortown. Hagen, as I have said, helped to establish this practice among his American fellow-professionals, for he was for thirty years their most influential leader. Most of the English players were still relying on the evidence of their eyes to judge distance. One might have expected some-one as relaxed as Hagen to do the same: when he had to, he could do it as well as any man. But when it was important, he added science to his flair. It is evidence again of that fascinating paradox of the shrewd golfing brain which lurked always beneath the playboy exterior.

He qualified easily enough, playing relaxed golf over the second of the qualifying rounds as it became obvious that he had nothing to fear.

On the first morning of the championship, conditions were perfect for golf, with a hazy sun and the lightest of westerly winds. We were not off until the end of the day, playing with young Henry Cotton, and I had to watch a succession of good scores come in during the morning.

I watched Harry Vardon over his last few holes, but it was a painful experience. He was striking the ball beautifully and effortlessly, but his putting had gone completely; he was moving his body and chopping across the short ones. He shook his head with a sad smile as he came off the last green. Even as a boy, I felt the sadness which has come many times since at the sight of a great player in decline.

The Americans brought in a succession of good scores: Diegel and Barnes had 71s; Farrell a 72; Sarazen and Watrous 73s. Behind them, the Englishman Percy Alliss was playing even better. He had as true and sweet a swing as anyone, and he came in with a 69 to lead the championship by two shots.

By two o'clock, as the good scores accumulated, the black clouds had gathered and thunder was rumbling over the Forth. A sea of multicoloured umbrellas rose as Hagen and Cotton made ready, at last, to begin.

Mercifully, there was little rain, but the wind had freshened by the time we began the round.

Great and enthusiastic Scottish crowds followed Hagen, the reigning champion, as he set out on his attempt to win his fourth Open. I had watched many of the other players tee off before us. Almost all of them were white and drawn, grim-faced with determination. Hagen was as smiling and relaxed as he struck off and moved down the first fairway as if he had been playing a friendly.

And he remained as laid back as that, even when his title seemed to be disappearing over the first few holes. He began 5, 5, 4, 5, with the last of these being at a short hole. Then he fought back, saving par several times when it looked as though he might drop further shots. It was not a spectacular round, but he gave little away. In the most difficult conditions of a fairly easy golfing day, he compiled a 75. It was to be a springboard for the real assault to come.

On the eighth, which was known as Archer's Wood, I had an example of the way his active mind stored away golfing information. This was a sharp dog-leg to the right. He drove into what looked a perfect fairway position, but the wind swept him on to the far side of the fairway. He had to play a wood from there, and left it in the bunker which blocked his path to the flag.

It cost him a five. As we left the green, he looked back down the hole and said, 'I got it wrong there, Sonny. I should have driven right, into the rough: the crowds have trodden it down, so it's not as punishing as it should be. It's a better line to the green from there.' Notice that he said, 'I got it wrong,' not 'You' or even 'We'. I never knew him to blame me for a bad shot. That is a modern

34

fashion, and one to be deplored: the player is the expert, and ultimately he makes his own decisions.

In subsequent rounds, Walter Hagen did as he had suggested, steering his tee shot carefully into the trodden rough on the right of the dog-leg. In the second round, he bounced unluckily into a bunker, but his thinking was right, and proven to be so on the last day. From the trodden rough, he had an adequate lie, a better line, and a very much shorter shot than he would have had from the orthodox position on the fairway, to which most people still played.

At the end of that first day, I surveyed the list of leading scores anxiously. Percy Alliss, showing his mastery of links conditions, still led by two after that marvellous round of 69. Before the championship, the experts had forecast that no-one in this field of great players would break 70 round the tough old course.

Two of Hagen's American Ryder Cup colleagues had moved in behind Alliss: Leo Diegel was on 71 and Johnny Farrell on 72, where Abe Mitchell had joined him. My man was lying no higher than twelfth; more important, he was six shots off the lead. I was young enough to shake my head among the other caddies and feel that it was too much. Hagen was back in the bar of the Marine Hotel: he had apparently scarcely studied the scores to see how he was placed.

'Remember the championship's over four rounds, Sonny!' was all he said, as he left my anxious face.

The second day of the championship was the best of the three for weather. There was not much blue sky or sun, but not much rain either. The clouds were high, the wind had dropped to a light breeze from the sea; the white horses were much less in evidence in the estuary of the river. 'A good day for golf,' said Walter Hagen as he joined me.

Because the first-round starting times were reversed, we were to be first off at 9 a.m. Hagen did his usual short but concentrated session with his putter on the practice green. Then he watched one of the players who was ahead of him on the leader board, but not due to tee off until an hour after him. He was on the practice area, smashing dozens of practice balls towards a distant caddie. 'If I had to work as hard as that to play golf, I'd find another way to make a living!' Hagen said, to whoever was listening.

Then he ambled across to the first tee and set about producing the greatest round of golf the Open had ever seen.

He was bunkered on the edge of the first green, but he almost holed from there. At the second, he pushed his drive, then played a second and third which were not very much better. He was a good twelve feet from the hole, but he ran the putt in as though it was a mere formality. Coming from the green with two fours which might have been fives, he grinned at me and said, 'Just what we needed, Sonny. Now let's go!'

And go he did. He holed another good putt for a three at the third, made his three at the tricky short fourth, where he had taken five in the first round and four in each of the qualifiers. Then, with a gentle wind behind him, he made a four look easy at the 500-yard fifth. It seemed almost inevitable when he holed another good putt for a three at the sixth. He had his first piece of bad luck at the eighth, for his drive was struck perfectly from the tee, but it kicked into a bunker. That cost him a five, but two

36

beautiful woods to the ninth gave him a four, and he was out in 33.

The news of these heroics spread fast, and the large crowd who had followed us from the start had more than doubled as we turned for home. Hagen began back 4, 4, 4, 3, with two of the fours very nearly threes. On the fourteenth he played his finest shot of this great round, one I remember vividly to this day. He needed a spoon (3-wood) for his second, and to me the green looked out of reach even with that. But I stood behind and watched the ball fly straight as an arrow against the blue sky for the whole of its journey, covering the flag for 250 yards, until it came to rest nine feet away from it. The putt went in for a three, to a roar compounded of delighted amazement as much as appreciation.

That was five under fours, which was the way we counted in those days. On the short sixteenth, it was almost seven under, for his putt curled round the lip but refused to drop for a two. The seventeenth was out of reach in two, and he took five; that left him with a four at the last for an unheard-of 67.

His drive was just in the rough; he pitched his second very nearly into the hole itself, but it ran seven yards past. Where lesser men would have laid up, the Haig went for it. He almost made it, but he was left with a tricky three-and-a-half-footer back. He surveyed it for a couple of seconds – professionals did not dream of asking a caddie's advice in those days, unless he happened to be a local – then holed it nervelessly to be back in 34.

There was a massive roar from the crowd, the biggest I had ever heard. The volume came simply because there were so many of them: crowds in those days were not given to the raucous, partisan cheering which is a feature of modern championships, even in the face of a 67 which had been thought impossible round Muirfield.

Nor was information so freely available around the course. There were no leader boards, except off the course by the eighteenth, and no boards were carried round with each group. But the news of this round flashed quickly back down the course. Hagen was taking the old links by the scruff of its neck and shaking it. And his score at the front of the field was having its effect upon his rivals. Alliss slipped to a 76 and Farrell to a 75.

The crowd had grown ever larger around us, and the central figure's diminutive caddie had scurried ever more apprehensively as they pressed upon his heels. Spectators were not roped off and kept away from the players then: that was a development suggested many years later by Cotton. Hagen smiled his appreciation of the applause, chatted occasionally as he walked on after a shot, allowed me to get to his ball and put down the clubs before he sauntered up.

He was a great contrast to the modern American pro. He had generally 'seen' the shot he intended to play even before he reached his ball, so that he rarely hesitated over the selection of his club. 'Never hurry, never worry and always stop to smell the flowers along the way' was his summary of his approach to golf; but it did not mean that he was a slow player.

He was always strolling, but he never spent the time over the preliminaries of a shot which makes some of the modern professionals so painful to watch. As Bernard Darwin recorded of this round, 'Hagen was the first to start at nine o'clock, and by half-past eleven he had smashed Alliss's short-lived record with a 67, and lifted himself to the very forefront.'

On 9 May 1929 Hagen could do no wrong. When he missed a green (on this day there were only a couple, but he played intentionally short on three or four occasions) he got down in two. He had twenty-eight putts, but that was because he chipped so close on these occasions. I think he holed only two putts of longer than six feet in the whole of that remarkable round.

Because Hagen was the greatest fashioner of a golf shot I ever saw (only Ballesteros among the moderns can rival him), it all looked very easy. I was dimly aware that Cotton was playing fine golf amidst the excitement; he came in with a 73, which served only to put the greatness of Hagen's round in context.

That 67 was the finest round ever played thus far in the sixty-four Open Championships. I can hear the applause ringing still around the clubhouse as we came off the course.

For the modern reader, that score needs to be put in context. Rounds of below 70 were then very rare. Hagen himself had had a 68 at Royal Lytham in 1926, and Bobby Jones a 68 at St Andrews in 1927. These were still spoken of with awe, and no-one had thought that score could be beaten around Muirfield.

The round was played with hickory shafts, and no great reliance on long hitting. In the years to come, I would see Cotton hit the ball with raw power, carrying it much greater distances than Hagen. There were many fairway wood shots in Hagen's round that day. But that only made his control of the ball the more remarkable. The nearer he got to the green, the more absolute that control became; once he was within fifty yards of the flag, he did not once fail to get down in two. Apart from Cotton's famous

39

round at Sandwich in 1934, Hagen's score that day was not to be surpassed in the Open for twenty-one years.

When the excitement had died down at the end of the day, I checked the full list of scores. Amidst the euphoria over the Haig's score, Leo Diegel's fine 69 to add to his opening 71 had not had the attention it deserved. His 140 for the opening two rounds was the lowest thirty-six-hole score the Open had ever seen, equalling Jones's total at St Andrews when he went on to win by six shots in 1927.

So the competition was intense, and Hagen was still not in the lead. But he had made up the ground I had been worried about after the first day, and was lying second. There were six Americans in the top eight. The leading thirty-six-hole scores were:

Leo Diegel	140
Walter Hagen	142
Abe Mitchell	144
Percy Alliss	145
Johnny Farrell	147
Bobby Cruickshank	147
Gene Sarazen	147
Johnny Golden	147

There is one interesting footnote to that remarkable round. Although I subsequently played to a handicap of four, I could never come anywhere near to Hagen as a golfer. But my memory is a lot better than his! In his autobiography, written twenty-seven years later, he gets a little of the detail wrong; more importantly, he claims this round stood as the lowest in the Open until Fred Daly's 66 at Troon in 1950. He has overlooked, of course, Henry

Cotton's remarkable round at Sandwich five years later. But then I *should* remember that, since I was also a humble assistant at the feast on that occasion.

In 1929, and for twenty-six years afterwards, two rounds were played on the last day of the Open. Nor did the leaders go off last, giving them the advantages of playing with each other and knowing what the players ahead of them had scored. That had to wait for the first television transmission, in 1957. The field was cut for these final rounds to sixty-four: fifty-eight pros and six amateurs.

I arrived early and studied the starting times, which I already knew by heart from the previous evening. Gene Sarazen was first off at 8.30. Abe Mitchell and Percy Alliss were paired together at 8.54. We were off at 9.18, paired with Henry Cotton. Leo Diegel, the leader, was not due off until almost two hours later.

The place was buzzing with a story of Hagen. Still carousing in the bar of the Marine Hotel at well past midnight, he had been reminded of the need for rest in preparation for the taxing thirty-six holes on the morrow. He acknowledged the thought politely and took no action. Rather desperately, his well-wisher pointed out to him the conscientious precautions of the only man ahead of him in the championship: 'But, Walter, Leo Diegel's been in bed now for three hours!'

The Haig eyed his friend for a moment with a smile. 'He might be in bed. But he sure-to-God ain't sleeping!' he said. Then he turned back to his glass and his friends for another hour.

Hagen himself has described the conditions at Muirfield as we made ready for the last two rounds:

The whitecaps topped huge rollers in the Firth of Forth, the wind whipped around us as we struggled to maintain a stance for a shot, and grabbed each ball fiercely as the shot was played. It was simply impossible to hit the ball and feel any assurance it would finish anywhere near the spot you'd aimed for . . . I decided to use the ground route whenever I could, for against the wind my ball was simply held in the air, with no control and no distance at all. The fairways were hard and fast, and a ball hit close to the ground would roll a great distance, and would conceivably avoid the wind.

There was no sign of a hangover as he joined me. He would never admit it – in modern parlance, he had an image to keep up – but on important occasions at least, he never seemed to drink as much as those around him. He loved company, and he liked the food and drink which went with it, but I never saw him drunk when there was golfing work to be done. He once told me that he had killed hundreds of pot plants with the drinks he quietly tipped away. He was not usually so unchivalrous as to turn away a lady, of course.

On this morning, he had the light of battle in his eye. I saw for the first time in my young life one of the things which makes a great champion. He was positively looking forward to the day, whilst others were apprehensive about it. He stood for a moment looking out over the grey rollers, then turned towards the course. 'Two seventy-fives should do it today, Sonny!' he said. He went away to wrap himself in sweaters, leaving me thinking that he was delighted with the harsh conditions.

But then I suspect he would have made himself

delighted with whatever conditions prevailed on that day. That was probably part of the psychology he applied to himself. For once, he could hardly wait to get on the course.

When we did, he was as good as his word. He hit the ball low when the wind was against or across us, choosing the straighter-faced club whenever there was a dilemma. He never strained for distance, preferring to be straight and short rather than risk going off line. It sounds simple enough, but the scores of others showed just how skilled were the things that Hagen was doing.

Cotton struck the ball well enough: on a calm inland course he would have scored well. But the wind, not he, determined where it came to rest. And where the Haig constantly rolled three shots into two around the greens, Cotton – who was almost invariably playing from much trickier places – could not do so. It was the first time that young Cotton had qualified for the last two rounds of the Open, and his scores were blown to oblivion on that wild Muirfield day: he had 82 and 80, to finish twenty-two strokes behind Hagen. But he was a quick and willing learner, and he would be back before long with his challenge.

Hagen had determined to learn how to handle links golf after his disastrous finish in his first Open in 1920. Now, in conditions which provided a supreme test, he showed his mastery of the techniques required. His stance was habitually a little wider than those of most of the moderns. Now he widened it still further, concentrating on the firm base which was essential to hit the ball at all in those conditions, punching the ball low to where he wanted it to go with his arms and a lot of right hand.

He ignored everyone else's score – 'Don't tell me,

Sonny, we've got our own problems' – and concentrated on his own battle with the elements. When he dropped a shot, he took it philosophically and looked to the next challenge. I found that Percy Alliss and Abe Mitchell, who had begun twenty-four minutes before us, were having trouble ahead of us. At about the same moment, Hagen had played the first six holes in one under fours, and I knew that he was in control.

At the seventh, he had a horrid plugged lie in a bunker. Instead of gently stroking the ball out in his usual manner (bunker shots required a wonderful touch and precision in the days before the sand wedge) he had to slash at it very hard and risk disaster. He not only got it out, but very nearly holed the putt for a three.

He got a great cheer when he completed the outward nine in 37. We had the biggest gallery on the course by far. It was partly because of the Haig's stupendous 67 on the previous day, but also in part, I am sure, because many Scots had come to see the cocksure American get his comeuppance in these conditions which were so foreign to him. When he proved supreme in the wind and rain which were blowing away so many of their own favourites, they were generous in their acknowledgement of his greatness. Hagen remarked afterwards that the thousands who lined the fairways and the greens provided him with a blanket against the wind, whenever he could keep the ball low enough.

As we turned with heads low into the fierce wind, he said to me, 'We've got the basis of our score, Sonny. Now we've got to hang on!' For the rest of the round, he showed that he could do just that, even when the putts which had been dropping on the Thursday refused obstinately to go in.

There were, of course, setbacks. He started back 4, 4, 5, but was then threatened with disaster at the short thirteenth. He punched in one of the low shots he had been playing so well, cut it just too fine, and caught the edge of the bunker. Then, with an awkward stance and the gale threatening to blow him over as he played, he chipped it out to about fifteen feet, and holed the putt.

After a poor second, he had a six on the fourteenth, when the wind wobbled a putt that I thought was going into the centre of the hole away to the edge of it and it stayed out. Head down against the wind, which threatened to swing me off my feet when it caught the big bag on my shoulder, I glumly added another two over fours to the score I was keeping in my head, but Hagen promptly made a glorious three at the fifteenth, with an iron shot punched dead straight into the teeth of the wind. He finished solidly with 4, 4, 5, and made for the welcome shelter of the clubhouse. He had the 75 he had aimed at when he set out upon the round: 37 out and 38 back.

While my golfer used all the time available for rest and sustenance, I grabbed what food I could before going to check on the progress of the rest of the field. There was no provision made for caddies, who looked after themselves as best they could. A shed opposite the Marine Hotel sold excellent pies, but it sold them to anyone. We took our places in the queue and worked our way slowly forward. Hunger as always was the best sauce, but I had little time to savour my lunch when I eventually handed over my pennies; I had to cram my pie down quickly whilst I hurried back to check the scores.

My heart leaped at what I saw. Of the leaders who were in, Hagen had posted the best score with his 75. Percy Alliss had 76 for 221, Johnny Farrell a 76 for 223. Sarazen

45

had scored 81, Cruickshank 78. Of the Americans that day, only Farrell came anywhere near to Hagen in mastering the wind – and he had begun five shots behind him. But the British golfers could do no better. The truth was that Hagen's 75 was a wonderful score in that wind.

There remained the leader at the beginning of the day, Leo Diegel. He was only just completing his round, and I went to check on his score as he left the eighteenth green. My heart was joyous, as maybe it should not have been at another's ill fortune. (But I was only sixteen!) Perhaps, as the Haig had suggested, poor Diegel had not been able to sleep after his early retirement. He had taken 82 shots for his third round.

Diegel had a remarkable putting style, with both elbows stuck out at right angles. It was an early method of keeping the arms rigid on the stroke, and he was generally highly successful with the putter. Imitators of his method could still be seen among elderly golfers until quite recently. But on this occasion his round had come apart on the greens: he had eight three-putts on this last day, an unheard-of thing for him. It was partly because he was not able to control the ball well enough in the wind to get near the hole; long putts through the gale were something of a lottery on the very fast greens.

All this meant that Hagen was taking out a four-stroke lead as we set off for the last round. For the first time he was in the lead, which brings a different kind of problem when the prize is so great. A lesser golfer, even perhaps a younger one, with things still to prove to himself and others, would have been tempted to defend his position, to be less positive than he had been when coming from behind in the morning.

Hagen's attitude altered not one iota. 'We're playing

the course, Sonny,' he said, perhaps reminding himself, as well as me, of the fact. 'Never mind how the others are going, let's just make sure this wind doesn't beat us.'

For seven holes, he did just that, whilst I collected the news of those in front and kept it to myself. Abe Mitchell was out in 40, Percy Alliss in 41. That meant that two of the main dangers were gone, for at the moment when the news came Hagen was completing his first seven holes in two under fours.

Then, at the eighth, he had the crowd moved back and played right as he had planned into the rough, cutting off most of the dog-leg and leaving himself a short iron to the green. It seemed that most of the last-day crowds were now following our match, sensing that history was in the making. When Hagen holed his six-footer, there was a great roar of approval.

When he returned to the course several years later, many of the locals had dubbed that eighth 'Hagen's hole'. But when he looked to play it in the same way, he found that the Committee had planted a clump of bushes in the right-hand rough, to prevent anyone playing there from the tee deliberately. The Honourable Company of Edinburgh Golfers as well as the Haig proved themselves quick learners!

Golf has a way of hitting back at any sign of complacency, whether one is a great player or a duffer. On the ninth, with the wind blowing across and against, Hagen lost control of a shot, for one of the few times on that wild day. It was his second shot, and the fates immediately compounded his error to put him in real trouble. His ball had hooked away to the left on the wind; when it bounced, it kicked further left, and came to rest within six inches of the stone wall which bounds the left of the hole. 'It was my own

47

fault,' said Hagen affably to the spectators who commiserated at his elbow as we went to investigate the damage. Concentration never necessitated silence for the Haig.

It was the kind of situation where I had seen the members at Moortown get into all kinds of trouble, usually because they attempted the impossible instead of declaring the ball unplayable and taking the penalty. Hagen now played the kind of shot they envisaged but never brought off. He played a left-handed shot, with a full swing. You can see how well-balanced he was when he completed his left-hand swing, as well as a little of my amazement, in the photograph of the stroke on page 3 of the picture section.

He hit the ball far better than anyone could have imagined. It went through the green, and although he chipped back to six feet, this time the putt did not go in. The hole cost him a six, but it could have been worse. Conditions had not improved: if Hagen could hold on and avoid disasters, he would win.

He did just that. His sixes at the fourteenth in the morning and the ninth in the afternoon were his only scores over five, on a day when the cards of the best were sprinkled with disasters. Throughout the day, his putting held, when that of most of the others was being buffeted away.

Hagen, whose career was built in an age when match-play dominated, even in the United States, was the best pressure putter I ever saw. His confidence never wavered, and that tells more in putting than in any other aspect of the game.

At the fourteenth, as if to atone for his morning six, he got a marvellous four, even though the hole was out of reach in two shots to everyone against that wild wind. He coasted home from there, knowing that barring miracles behind him he had the title within his grasp for a fourth time.

In due course, we came a little wearily to the eighteenth, and Hagen holed out carefully before a huge gallery. He had made his second 75 of that rough but memorable day, doing exactly what he had set out to do seven hours earlier. (The starting times allowed over an hour for lunch, and we were finished before four o'clock; so you can see how long it took Hagen to play the last two rounds of the world's greatest championship, threading his way through crowds not kept behind ropes.)

We had to wait for everyone to come in, but I knew then that he had won. In the end, his total of 292 meant that he had taken his fourth Open by no fewer than six shots, with Farrell second and Diegel third. Americans had filled the first three places and continued their domination of the championship. Eventually, the young Englishman who had suffered alongside Hagen would do something about that. But that was only after another five years of strenuous effort.

The old claret jug and the winner's cheque for £100 were presented to Hagen by Mr A. W. Robertson-Durham. The triumvirate of British golfing greats, Harry Vardon, James Braid and J. H. Taylor, winners between them of sixteen Opens, all came and shook his hand and complimented him on his play that day.

When the speeches and the congratulations were over and the crowds were beginning to melt away, Hagen turned to me, 'Well, Sonny, we did it.'

'Yes, Mr Hagen.' He turned over the envelope containing the cheque in his large hands. Then he handed it to me. 'You'd better have this, Sonny. It's my fourth Open, and you deserve the reward.'

And so he passed his winning cheque straight to his caddie. I gulped, but I was not quite dumbfounded. 'You have endorsed it, haven't you, Mr Hagen?' I gasped.

Fortunately, although Bob Harlow, Hagen's manager, made sure that the Press were well aware of the champion's gesture, the native caution of his Yorkshire caddie was not reported!

I had never seen so much money as was represented by that single piece of paper. It was worth well over a hundred times what it would be now. For Hagen, it implemented his philosophy that he did not want to be a millionaire, only to live like one. Of course, he knew that the appearance money that Open titles guaranteed him was far greater than the prize money itself. But he didn't just talk as though he did these generous things; he actually did them.

And for the recipient in the depressed Britain of 1929, it was riches beyond his wildest dreams. I bought my mother a cowhide suite which she had looked at wistfully for months. It cost £17. Sixty-four years later, my sister has it still in use, and it looks good for another sixty-four.

I travelled back with Maurice Hart, paying for our charabanc tickets from Newcastle to Leeds in lordly fashion out of my winnings. 'What next, Ernest?' he said, as we climbed stiffly out with our cases in Leeds.

'I'm caddying for Hagen for the rest of his time in Britain,' I said loftily. 'He was a bit vague, but I know he's in two or three tournaments. And I think he's in demand to play with dukes and people like that.'

Maurice probably thought I was pushing it a bit, and perhaps I was. But in fact, it turned out I had been underestimating a little.

50

CHAPTER FOUR

HIGH LIVING AND
HIGH SOCIETY

THE UNREAL SUMMER WHICH HAD BEGUN WITH MY IMPULSIVE action in seizing Walter Hagen's bag at Moortown continued through July and August. I met him now by appointment at a succession of courses, taking the familiar big bag reverently from the Rolls-Royce he had hired to tour the country.

We came back to Moortown for the *Evening News* tournament. This was a match-play tournament, like many of the important ones in the twenties. But to get the field down to a manageable size, there were thirty-six holes of stroke play to determine who would qualify.

Playing in his usual relaxed and chatty style, Hagen led the qualifiers. As he said to me, 'There's no prize for coming first in this, Sonny.' Once he was sure he had done enough to qualify, he was not particularly concerned about his position in the list; but as usual he gave good value to the crowds who had paid to see him. As often

51

happens when it does not particularly matter, a good score came easily.

But that did not ensure an easy draw. There was no seeding, and the best players were as likely to meet in the first round as to be kept apart until the later stages. Hagen was drawn against the man who had given him such a thrashing in the Ryder Cup a few weeks previously, George Duncan. Of course, since then, Hagen had triumphed convincingly in the Open at Muirfield, and Duncan had trailed in a long way behind him.

But that is not quite the same as the head-to-head confrontation of match-play, and the Press was full of talk of a 'revenge match' for the Ryder Cup defeat. Both men played well, at the cracking pace which Duncan enjoyed; both of them, I am sure, enjoyed the match. They had had some notable encounters before. Duncan had been second by one stroke after a magnificent last-round 69 when Hagen won his first Open at Sandwich in 1922. And he had prevailed more often than not in their match-play meetings.

There had been much drama in their matches, and this one was to be no exception. The score ebbed and flowed, with rarely more than one hole in it over the thirty-six holes. When they came to the last, they were both on the green in two, with outside chances of birdies. Hagen putted first, and for a moment I, and most of the crowd, thought he had holed it. But his ball rimmed the hole, and left Duncan with what was almost a dead stymie.

The stymie remained for twenty-three years after this an important part of golf. Although it never seemed fair to me, it was regarded as an important part of the match-play ethos, an indication that 'the rub of the green' was a thing which all golfers had to accept.

52

If the ball which was blocking your route was some distance from the hole, it was usual to attempt a delicate chip shot, giving your ball just enough elevation to clear the obstacle and then allowing it to roll towards the hole. But where, as in this case, the ball blocking you was on the edge of the hole, no such ploy was possible. I expected Duncan to play safely up to the side of the hole, accept his half, and go on to extra holes. If he tried to do more, he risked knocking in Hagen's ball and conceding the match to a three.

He did not even appear to think about it. As was his custom, he stepped up to his putt almost before Hagen's ball had stopped rolling. It was a putt of perhaps twelve feet, and as soon as he hit it I realized that he was attacking the cup, not playing for a half. His ball rolled quite rapidly towards the one on the edge of the hole, looking until the very last moment as if it was going to knock it in and give Hagen the match.

When it was about to hit it full on, it moved perhaps an inch to the left with the borrow of the green, flicked the side of Hagen's ball, caught the very edge of the hole, and rattled in.

There was a collective gasp, then an enormous roar from the crowd. It took me a moment to grasp that Hagen had lost the match, when it had seemed impossible for him to do so. He was smiling and shaking hands with the delighted Duncan, whilst I already had his bag across my shoulders, ready to move on to the first tee to continue the match.

In August Hagen and Duncan were both made honorary members of Moortown, in recognition of their captaincies of their respective Ryder Cup teams. This honour, accorded by such an exclusive club, delighted

Hagen. He still remembered his first visit to Deal in 1920, when he had been refused entry to the clubhouse and smartly despatched to change in the professional's shop.

Duncan's *tour-de-force* putt at Moortown left Hagen out of the tournament, but not without employment. Bob Harlow, who arranged his itinerary in Britain, had been besieged at Muirfield with offers of exhibition matches. He was always behind the first tee when Hagen was due off, doing sponsorship deals, arranging appearances, giving the Press the quotes from Hagen which made him such splendid copy throughout his career.

I suppose Harlow was the Mark McCormack of his day, but things were less formal and organized in the twenties; in an era of fewer restrictions, the opportunities for a golfing entrepreneur were almost limitless. Hagen realized this, trusted Harlow, and gave him his head. As he recalled much later: 'I realized I needed a manager-press-agent and I found him in the person of Bob Harlow. He knew his business and he grew to know me – my good points and my shortcomings. Through all those years we never had a written contract of any sort. He set up the dates, I played the tournaments and exhibitions. And we carried the greenbacks away in an old suitcase. It was an ideal arrangement, for it allowed me to enjoy my friends and my game.'

Hagen was certainly good at that. 'Don't worry me about the money, Bob,' he said, as we journeyed about the country. 'Just pay the bills and keep it coming!' And Harlow did. As in America, he carried a suitcase of banknotes, adding to its contents as the tour went along, dispensing from it to meet the considerable expenses of hotel and bar bills. Britain was more staid than the United States, and in the middle of a recession, but it still offered rich pickings. 'We'll go anywhere, if the price is right!' Harlow would grin when people came forward tentatively, half-expecting to be refused.

He was as good as his word. If the money was right and the time was available, Hagen went. He did not play exclusively at the great courses, as modern professionals – millionaires already from their prize money and advertising endorsements – usually do. One of the ironies of this is that it was Walter Hagen more than any man who put the modern professional golfer in the affluent position he now enjoys.

Of course the tournament circuit then was not so fully developed as now – hence the need for all British professionals to have secure club jobs. The organization of the game was still geared to the amateur ethos – remember that two of Jones's famous 'grand slam' of titles in 1930 were amateur championships. But the greatest Americans, thanks to Hagen's example, were already making a living from simply playing high-quality golf.

In the weeks after the Open, we visited some fairly obscure courses, just because the price had been right and Harlow had struck deals with them. He refused some famous names because they felt they had the right to the great man's presence without paying the going rate. But Bob Harlow, like his master, was never averse to ruffling a few feathers. I occasionally witnessed Harlow's negotiations at first hand, and to a sixteen-year-old who had never been able to say anything but 'Yes, sir' to the demands of such people, they gave a thrill of horrified delight.

And wherever we went, Hagen enjoyed himself. He would look at a nondescript course, eye the blue sky and the surrounding trees appreciatively, and say, 'Well, here's a chance to sink a few putts and a few drinks.' Invariably he did both. And just as invariably Bob Harlow, who insisted on cash, was packing more notes away in his case at the end of the day.

And the comet to whose tail I had attached myself took the fatherless lad from Leeds into some strange places, socially as well as geographically.

Sir Philip Sassoon had already invited Hagen to bring the American Ryder Cup team to his estate at Trent Park in Middlesex. They had stayed there when they landed in England, practising on his private course as they prepared for the contest at Moortown.

Now Hagen went back there to play with his friends. The Duke of Kent was among them, and titles were plentiful. The hospitality flowed liberally, and I saw how people like butlers, whom I had never seen before, conducted themselves and behaved towards their masters. I had no idea of it at the time, but it was all to prove valuable learning for the wide-eyed youth looking on from the sidelines and trying to merge into the abundant greenery.

On a bright day at the end of July, we travelled to the exclusive Swinley Forest Club, near Ascot. Aubrey Boomer was to partner Sir Philip Sassoon in a 'greensome' against Hagen and partner. No-one had thought to inform me in advance who that partner might be. It turned out to be the Prince of Wales.

The future King Edward was a very keen golfer. He had followed Hagen over the last nine holes of his 1928 Open triumph at Sandwich and presented him with the trophy afterwards. He had taken lessons from many of the leading professionals in Europe. Archie Compston had been his private instructor for a number of years, accompanying him on numerous trips to the Continent.

The course was closed to members for the match, and guards followed us round at a discreet distance, not to protect the Prince, but to keep away the curious. They hauled a cameraman out of the bushes near the fourth green. I wondered whether he would be sent to the Tower or summarily executed on the course, but he was merely sent away with a flea in his ear, without even losing his camera.

Prince Edward was already on good terms with Hagen, and of course he chose to have the Open champion as his partner. 'Greensomes', wherein both players drive and then choose which ball to play for the rest of the hole, is a good game for the expert to mix with the not-so-expert, since any really bad drive can be discarded.

I do not recall many of those from the Prince. He was a competent player, fairly orthodox, as one would expect from someone who had received much instruction, but without any great length. Hagen says that his partner drove 225 yards down the middle on the second hole, but I am sure he is a little generous. I do not remember any of the royal shots ever being so long, and I too was on his side!

However, he played steadily enough for a man whose handicap was about fourteen. The Haig was not quite at his best, and found that when he was off line, the heather in this fine belt of golfing country was very punishing. But he played some typical recovery shots over the last few holes, and the illustrious pair won one up. After a buffet lunch in the clubhouse, Hagen gave his partner a lesson. He actually got the Prince hitting his iron shots from the inside, with a little draw, and the future King Edward departed as delighted with his day as any other golf-crazy amateur.

At the end of the British season, Hagen prepared to depart for the Paris Open. 'Come with me to France, Sonny, and see the sights of Paris!' said the Haig. I was more alarmed than excited. To an inexperienced lad of sixteen, the fleshpots of the legendary city of pleasure seemed threatening rather than enticing. 'I – I don't think I can, Mr Hagen,' I said. 'I'm expected home, you see. And I've got to start thinking about a job.'

He teased me a little, but didn't press me too hard. Perhaps he saw how young I was still under the careless exterior I tried to project; perhaps he felt that if he took me off abroad he would have a responsibility for me. As he always said, he wasn't good at responsibilities.

If the truth were known, I think I was rather more homesick than I cared to admit. All this had begun with a day out to see if I could pick up a player's bag for a Ryder Cup practice day at Moortown. It had taken me all over the country with the most famous golfer of his age, set me beside champions and princes. I still thought each day that if I pinched myself I would wake up. I had better get home before I did so.

Hagen paid me handsomely, and I had been frugal in my spending; I had plenty of money left after I bought my train ticket from London to Leeds. My last view of Hagen was as he mounted the steps to the Savoy Hotel. Fred Corcoran, baggage master to the American Ryder Cup team, was supervising the removal of the great man's clubs from the boot of the Rolls.

As usual, there was a considerable reception committee for Hagen, who proceeded royally among them. He turned round on the top step of the Savoy entrance and stopped a moment before disappearing through the doors to the brilliantly lit luxury he loved. 'Goodbye, Sonny!' he called. 'Look after yourself!'

I trudged through the darkening streets to King's Cross Station. The world seemed suddenly much smaller.

CHAPTER FIVE

DEPRESSION AND A NEW START

I CAME DOWN TO EARTH WITH A BUMP WHEN I GOT HOME.

The country was slipping towards the great slump of the early thirties, and each week the number of unemployed in Leeds grew. The family were pleased, even impressed, by my tales of the summer I had enjoyed, but it was time to get back to the real world, they said. Being a caddie had been fun, but it was a part-time occupation, as well as a precarious one.

Reluctantly, I had to agree. Being an all-the-year-round caddie for one player was then unheard-of. With no established circuit, all the British professionals needed their club teaching jobs to be sure of a living for themselves. Hagen was blazing a trail in America, and young Henry Cotton was watching with interest, but the circumstances were not yet right for a golfing circus on similar lines in Britain.

Many of the best British players went to fashionable

continental clubs, which were prepared to pay them more than most of the ones in Britain. Aubrey Boomer was at St-Cloud in Paris. Abe Mitchell travelled about with Sam Ryder as his personal professional. Henry Cotton, brightest hope of British golf, went eventually to Waterloo in Belgium for three years. The professionals themselves had to work hard to make a living, as memberships of golf clubs fell in the thirties. For caddies, the world was bleaker still.

Modern golfers, accustomed to long waiting lists and ever-rising subscriptions, may be surprised to hear that all but a few élite golf clubs were anxious about their futures in the thirties. Many of them conducted brisk recruiting drives, encouraging their existing members to bring in new faces, but they were not always successful.

Most clubs of the stature of Moortown had a few regular caddies for their members. But they were considered – and I'm afraid for the most part were – a disreputable lot. There was no question of my mother allowing me to join their dubious ranks; that was just as well, for the wheeled caddie cart, which would destroy the precarious living of most of the full-time caddies, was almost at hand.

I had to turn my hand to 'real' work.

My mother secured for me what was considered a great boon in those hard times. I was apprenticed as a tailor at Burton's, where she was now a trusted worker of long standing.

There was keen competition for apprenticeships. A trade was considered the best passport to employment for life. A skilled man, they said, would never be long out of work. His services would be always in demand, and he would be able to take his expertise elsewhere if a particular job did not suit him.

It was an appealing idea, even a logical one: surely those with a long and specialized training would be in an excellent position to sell their services? It had been so, generally speaking, in the days of full employment. But it was the inability of men who had 'served their time' to a trade to get work in the thirties which began the long decline of the apprentice system.

My days of learning were not well paid. The theory was that one would compensate for these lean years with better-than-average wages when fully qualified. For a sixteen-year-old beginning a four-year apprenticeship, those days seemed distressingly far away.

For the first two years of my apprenticeship at Burton's, I was paid 2s. 6d. (12½p) per week. In the third year, this doubled to 5s. (25p) per week. In the fourth and last year, I got the princely sum of 10s. (50p) per week.

Fortunately I supplemented this at weekends by caddying for the members at Moortown, often earning more than in the five days of my working week. I got 1s. (5p) for a round, or 1s. 6d. (7½p) for thirty-six holes. But I was something of an expert by this time, and the news of my summer of caddying for Hagen had spread discreetly among the members, so that I invariably got a tip as well as my fee at the end of the day.

Many good players came to Moortown, for big amateur competitions as well as professional tournaments. I was usually able to secure a bag on such occasions. That pleased me, for I felt I was continuing to learn about golf as well as maintaining my caddie status.

And each year I arranged my meagre holidays to coincide with the week of the Open. Because of the thirty-six holes of qualifying and the practice days, I was not able to get there early enough to try for a player's bag. In any case, after the Haig, almost anyone else would have seemed an anticlimax. Hagen did not come again for four years: after his Muirfield title in 1929, he won no more of the great championships.

But I saw Bobby Jones, still looking boyish in the year when he would retire, winning at Hoylake. I learned then about character in golf, for the great man, on his way to the grand slam which will never be repeated, was not at his best for much of the championship. Leading by a single stroke after two rounds, be began the third by dropping eight shots to par in the first three holes. I listened to the excited chatter in the crowd behind me: no-one could remember his ever doing that before. Yet he still came in with a 74 at lunch, preserving a slender one-stroke lead over Archie Compston.

In the afternoon, he negotiated those first three holes safely, in front of a crowd gathered in ghoulish antici-pation and hoping for an overdue home success. At the eighth, Jones was almost up in two, and we anticipated the birdie which would virtually clinch the title for him. From there, he took five more to get down, and seemed suddenly to have thrown everything away. But how he fought from there to the end, repeatedly making par when his normally impeccable swing had let him down!

He came in with a 75, good enough to win by two shots. I can see him now, smiling, but white-faced with exhaustion, holding aloft the trophy he would never compete for again and looking at it fondly against the blue sky. That picture of him at the height of his achievements came back to me always when I saw him in his later years, a great athlete with a crippling disease, cheerful and un-complaining in his wheelchair.

In 1931 I made my first visit to the great links at

Carnoustie. For a while, it seemed as if Percy Alliss might break the American domination of the Open, but in the end he was third, two strokes behind Tommy Armour. As in the previous year, four of the first six were from the United States. In 1932 Gene Sarazen, who had been close on several previous occasions, won at Prince's, Sandwich, by a clear five shots. It was a popular victory for the little man, who had sworn to keep coming back until he won; but we began to wonder if a Briton would ever win again.

We hoped it would happen at the home of golf in 1933, but Sid Easterbrook lost by a single stroke, and five of the first six were Americans. I saw Hagen again there. 'Hi, Sonny!' he said, as if he'd left me only a week before. 'How's things?' He sauntered round the course much as he always had, and for two rounds I was thrilled to see that his game seemed as magical as ever. After thirty-six holes, he led the field with 140.

The last day was windy, as it had been four years earlier at Muirfield, and I longed to be out there with the great man, carrying the big bag and bustling forward with head down against the wind. Alas, he tired visibly through the day, being now over forty and having lived life to the full. Despite a 79 in the morning, he was still tied for the lead with Denny Shute, the eventual winner after a play-off.

Had he been playing under the modern system of only one round a day, I believe he would have won his fifth Open. He would have slept more easily as joint leader than anyone else in the field! But he was blown right away in the afternoon, and finished a rather sad and tired twenty-second. I was still only twenty, but I sensed the end of an era. Later that year, Hagen announced his retirement from serious competition.

*　　*　　*

In 1934 I finished my apprenticeship at Burton's. I had been looking forward to the day, for that meant I would be paid a decent wage at last, as a fully qualified cutter and stitcher.

Instead, I got the sack! It was no-one's fault. Burton's were laying off workers who had been with them for years, because they were simply not selling enough suits in the depression to keep the work-force. They could not be expected to take on newly qualified men like me if it meant laying off old hands.

Nevertheless, the consequences for me were stark. I was a qualified tailor with nowhere to go: if Burton's were not selling suits at the bottom end of the market, business was certainly not expanding elsewhere. 'What are you going to do?' said my mother.

I sensed from her tone that she suspected what I had in mind. 'I shall go down to the Open as usual. And I'll see what I can pick up there.'

Her face clouded. 'You need to be around here, seeing if there's anything available for a qualified man.'

'Ma, you know there's nothing for me in Leeds at the moment. I know a lot of influential people in golf now. Everyone who matters in golf is around at the Open. I know where they'll be staying in Sandwich, because I was there in 1928 when they last played there. I might just pick something up, now that I know I can look for it.'

It was all true enough. I had really nothing to lose; but I'm still not sure that I was not just making excuses because I wanted to see the Open. And I was twenty now; whatever her misgivings, my mother hesitated to interfere with my plans, and in golf, at least, she conceded that I knew a little more than she did. I reminded her that in my

65

one well-recalled summer with Walter Hagen, I had earned more than in the entire four-year period since.

On the long journey to the south, I formulated my plans. When I got off the train in Kent, I made for the one British golfer I thought might win for us, after ten successive American victories. After all, Walter Hagen had told me, 'Sonny, you must always aim higher than you think you can reach.'

The man I had in mind was beginning to make a name for himself for his style off the course as well as his golf on it, just as Hagen had. He had been the first British golfer to imitate Hagen's two-tone golf shoes; he wore cashmere sweaters of the same quality; he was given to staying at the best hotels and arriving at courses in large limousines. As directly as I had gone for Hagen at Moortown as a sixteen-year-old in my school uniform, I now sought out the whereabouts of Thomas Henry Cotton.

I knew where I would find him. In many important respects, he was the antithesis of Hagen as a golfer. He was, for instance, an almost obsessive practiser, who had privately dedicated himself to winning the Open and planned his schedule each year to take account of that. This was a practice day, two days before the championship. I was certain that T. H. Cotton (Waterloo) would be somewhere on the course.

I was right. I found him easily enough, but I was sensible enough to keep well clear until he had completed the hole he was playing. He was intensely serious on the course, never speaking to anyone in case it disturbed his concentration. I had watched him often enough, and read much more. Even though he was now only practising, I did not risk disturbing that formidable concentration.

In those pre-war days, there were no charges and no prohibitions on practice days. As I followed at a respectable distance, I saw that the young man (he was only six years older than I was) appeared to have a depressingly large retinue of followers around him. He recognized me as he came off the eighteenth green. 'Hello, young Hargreaves,' he said.

He knew me, of course, from the Ryder Cup at Moortown and the Open at Muirfield, where he had struggled ineffectively to match Hagen's brilliance in the last two rounds. And we had spoken briefly at other Opens since, but I was absurdly pleased that he should know my name.

'Hello, Mr Cotton.' I took a deep breath. 'Have you got a caddie for the Open?'

'I'm afraid I have. Ernest Butler here is caddying for me.' He gestured towards a quiet, elderly figure behind him, who gave me a measured but not unfriendly nod. Perhaps Butler admired my cheek: it was a necessary quality in caddies who wished to secure regular work.

Possibly Cotton saw my disappointment. I think he knew what an enthusiast I was for this infuriating game, and that always weighed heavily with him. As I turned heavily away, he said, 'Look here. You could earn a few shillings by acting as a forecaddie for me if you like. Watch for my ball in front, and check on how the other players are doing for me.'

Fortunately for me, there was then no rule restricting a player to one caddie; if there had been, I should have gone back to Leeds and the dole. 'I'll do that, Mr Cotton.' My eagerness amused some of those who had been following the great man, but I did not care about that.

'Good. Just check when my starting times are, and we'll see you on the first tee on Monday.'

I went away, walking on air, to find myself some accommodation. I did not know it, but I had begun an association that would last for over forty years.

CHAPTER SIX

THE OPEN OF 1934

I HAD NOTICED ONE THING IN MY BRIEF VIEWING OF COTTON on the practice day. He was playing well.

An apocryphal story has been spread that he was playing so badly in the days before the championship that he considered withdrawing. It is a good newspaper rumour, which was not taken seriously even at the time by my friends among the golf reporters. No-one who knew Cotton and his obsession with the Open would have considered such a suggestion seriously. It is true that he brought several sets of clubs with him to the practice days, but by the time I arrived on the Saturday afternoon, he was striking the ball solidly and confidently.

He took Sunday off. This again has been misinterpreted. He did so beause he was confident of his readiness for the fray, not because he was in despair. It was his habit to rest on the eve of the Open, doing little or no practice: this was the most demanding golfing week of the year, and he was careful to preserve his physical resources for the most important part of it.

When the world's Press poured in and the great players of the world flexed their muscles for the first day of the 1934 Open, Cotton continued to play well. I do not use the word 'great' lightly: in over sixty years of contact with the world's best, I would accord the epithet to only eight or nine players, some of whom I discuss in a later chapter of this book. One of the things that distinguishes them is an ability to take promising form in practice into the tournament proper.

The bigger the occasion, the more difficult it is to do that. There is much superstition among golfers, as among other sportsmen; you will often hear modern golfers wondering if they are playing too well just before a championship, whether they have 'peaked too early'. One did not hear that particular nervous tic so often in the past; but then the circuits of professional tournaments were neither so continuous nor under such relentless media scrutiny as the modern ones.

Conversely, that made the sense of occasion for the really big contests like the Open even greater. There were more pressmen in Sandwich than one saw in the rest of the year put together: I knew all the regulars by now, but they were supplemented by assistants, whose duty was to relay the latest scores on the course back to their leaders as they waited by telephones. Evening newspapers were then in their heyday; there was no television, and radio was still in its infancy. There was great competition to provide the most up-to-date scores, with the smudged print of the 'Stop Press' space having its own suggestion of drama which was almost literally 'hot from the press'.

Henry Cotton had put a certain amount of pressure

upon himself. He had made no secret of the fact that it was his ambition to wrest this oldest and greatest of major titles from the Americans, who had now held it continuously for ten years. Cotton had played in all but the first of those years, beginning when he was still an eighteen-year-old assistant at Rye.

In retrospect, those years may be seen as the essential learning process, the springboard which enabled him to become not only Open Champion but the greatest British golfer of his era. In 1929 I had seen him struggling over the last thirty-six holes in the wind of Muirfield, which Hagen had mastered so well to win. He had led after the first round with Bobby Jones at Hoylake in 1930. In 1931 he had led after two rounds at Carnoustie, but played too defensively in the third. In 1933 at St Andrews, he had been joint leader after three rounds but finished only as joint seventh, three shots behind the winner. But he learned from each experience: in the years to come, I would see at first hand just how fully he had assimilated and applied the lessons of those years.

But his single-mindedness led to some of that intensity which was to threaten his health in later years. As he wrote himself in 1948: 'My attempt to win the Open always started from the moment the preceding one was over, and I kept setting my target twelve months ahead to achieve a certain result on a certain course. I suppose this obsession to win the greatest title of them all made it all the more difficult for me, but it was foremost in my mind for years.'

In those days, the tension built for the players through the thirty-six holes of qualifying as it does not today. When one added the necessary practice days to the six rounds of play, the competition stretched to something of

71

a marathon. You had to be a fit man as well as a fine player to come to the final thirty-six holes of the Open fresh enough to play them well on the final day.

Cotton, starting early on the first day of qualifying, thought he had played 'eighteen of the most perfect holes I have ever played.' He was objective, not immodest, in that assessment. It was the most faultless exhibition I had ever seen. *The Times* wrote:

> Cotton proceeded to play such golf as had never been seen on the links . . . He had no hole over par; he had no hole over 4; and it may fairly be said that he made no bad or even poor shot. He was constantly putting for 3s when he got 4s and he made the game look almost laughably easy. Indeed, the spectators did laugh, rather hysterically, as every drive split the fairway and every approach shot ended within six or eight yards of the hole . . .
>
> The wind, which got up freshly from the south at about midday, only blew towards the end of Cotton's round. Still, making all due allowances, his was just about as fine a round as anyone has ever seen or could wish to see, and it was played, moreover, with just the right degree of seriousness and no more, and an entire and delightful absence of fretting and fuming.

Cotton was round in 66, smashing by two strokes the course record, which had stood for over twenty years. It was no wonder that there was speculation in the Press that the round had come just too early.

I found acting as a forecaddie more strenuous than I had anticipated. On that first day, there was not much difficulty with the system of semaphore signalling we used to tell Cotton the fate of his tee-shots; I think he missed only one fairway all day, and that by no more than five feet. But I had also to protect the ball against the casual feet of the spectators, who roamed at will across the fairways. I stood – a little officiously, I fear – with my umbrella defending the position of the ball until my man arrived. Then I hared off to stand near the green whilst he played his second.

If he hit the green, as on that first day he usually did, I would run back as he approached to tell him how near the flag he was. 'About ten feet, Mr Cotton,' I would say, in answer to his glance of enquiry. The only other person to speak to him was Ernest Butler, carrying his clubs with stately dignity: Cotton was the first golfer to aim unashamedly at that cocoon of concentration which most modern golfers strive for. Bobby Jones had concentrated hard on his game when I watched him in the twenties, but he always seemed slightly apologetic about it. Cotton was a tremendous contrast with the urbane and relaxed Walter Hagen, who now would come to our Open no more.

As they putted out, I would be securing my position on the next fairway, ready to spot my golfer's ball and secure its position against interference when he put it into play. It was a system which golfers would be allowed to use for several more years, though the rules would eventually be altered to allow each player only one caddie.

Cotton led by four shots at the end of the first day of qualifying. It was a pity that this brilliant round had been 'thrown away' before the championship, but it did make the second qualifying round no more than a formality. Even after a 75 at Deal on an unpleasantly sultry and occasionally wet second day, Cotton's 141 was only a stroke from leading the qualifiers.

In my garret room on the night of Tuesday, 26 June, I slept uneasily in the heat, waiting impatiently for the real battle to begin.

The course looked immaculate when I arrived. Sandwich had its own supply of water, and because it could drench the fairways as well as the greens, they were like verdant carpets, almost unique in those days in Britain, particularly at seaside courses. This meant that high shots stopped of their own accord on the greens, which was thought likely to suit the Americans in the field, like Sarazen and Shute, the holder, more than the British players.

I had a secret fear that this first round might be an anticlimax after Cotton's 66 on this course on the Monday. He quickly dispelled that thought when we set out in a pleasant light breeze, almost at the end of the field. He made an easy four at the first, then smashed his drive at the second far past the point where I had elected to stand, almost on to the green, and made his three.

Dallemagne, the Frenchman with whom he was playing, responded with some fine golf, and went to the turn in 33. It mattered not: Cotton, playing so well that it seemed almost impossible for him to drop a shot, played these first nine in an incredible 31.

He had to hole a good putt for his four at the tenth. Then, at the eleventh, he drove so far and so straight that he reached a bunker which we had all thought out of range: it cost him a five – the only time he was over par in the two rounds he had played over the course – but he at once had a three at the twelfth. Dallemagne fell away a little to a 38 home; as Bernand Darwin said, his 71 'would have appeared wholly magnificent in any other company'.

But he was with Cotton. The crowds, hungry for British success after the American domination, gathered steadily around us as the news of his score ran around the rest of the course. The twenty-seven-year-old English challenger did not fail them: he was back in level fours for a 67. He had broken the old course record for the second time, and led the field by three strokes.

He had also equalled the Open Championship record score, that same 67 which Walter Hagen had compiled with me as caddie five years earlier. This was the first time I had enjoyed a formal role in the great contest since then: I began to feel that I might be something of a lucky mascot. I hoped others would notice the connection!

Cotton was staying at the Guildford Hotel. So were four veterans with no fewer than seventeen Open titles between them, all anxious to see the championship return to Britain. They were Harry Vardon, J. H. Taylor and James Braid, the great triumvirate, and Ted Ray, who had won both the British and the American Opens. The unstinting support and encouragement of these players meant a lot to the young man who was so determined to win at Sandwich.

I had installed myself at the Admiral Owen pub behind the Guildford, this being the nearest I could position myself to the great man. It was noisy and busy, but I did not mind that, for it was full of the excitement of the Open, of which I now felt myself a part. I heard people talking about Cotton's chances, and restrained myself with difficulty from claiming my involvement with the man of the moment. The years of enforced silence as a caddie to the gentlemen of Moortown were bearing fruit!

I woke early on the second morning, checking nervously on the elements through my small square of window in the roof of the building. The sky was blue and the clouds high. People were sauntering on the seafront, enjoying a pre-breakfast stroll through the lightest of sea breezes. I had no time for such indulgences; after a swift bacon-and-egg breakfast, I hurried across to the Royal St George's Golf Club to find my golfer.

We were the fourth match off, at 9.42, but I was in good time as always. I envied Ernest Butler, who was ensuring that all was as it should be with his man's equipment; it felt strange for me to be waiting about with nothing of that sort to divert me.

It was almost an hour before Cotton stood by the first tee, talking with Taylor, Braid and Ray; Vardon was too ill to walk the full course with them. In the presence of these giants of the game, men passing already into the legend of golf, I stood so still that I became almost part of the scenery, afraid that if I was noticed I would be banished out of earshot.

They chatted a little about the other scores – Cotton was three ahead of the field – and agreed with him that he needed to keep attacking the course, thinking of his own game rather than anyone else's. There was nothing remarkable about the talk, which was conducted to keep Cotton relaxed rather than for its own sake. I was twenty-one now, arrived, as they used to say, at man's estate. But, officially permitted to stand in the very shadow of these golfing heroes ancient and modern, I experienced once more the familiar feeling that I might at any moment wake up and find myself in bed in Leeds.

There was nothing in the rest of the day to rid me of that feeling. Henry Cotton, with me rushing to his every tee-shot to demonstrate my zeal and assert my responsibility, produced the most remarkable round in the history of the Open.

There was no more than a pleasant breeze when we finally got under way. The first drive was wind-assisted; I positioned myself well down the fairway, but the ball almost reached me. Cotton needed only a spade mashie (the nearest modern club would be a 6-iron) to reach the green on this 441-yard hole. I moved a little further down the second, until the golfers stood silhouetted like toy soldiers on the distant tee. Cotton launched himself into an immense hit, and the ball bounced on and on over the fast green turf; it passed within five yards of me, then rolled twenty yards past the spot which I had thought it impossible to reach. There was a collective gasp from the crowd. George Greenwood, in the next day's *Daily Telegraph*, measured the drive at 300 yards. Such hitting was unheard of in the thirties.

I hurried to the ball, at which the spectators were peering in awe. Cotton had to wait for his companion professional to play from some seventy yards behind him. Then he played a gentle niblick (9-iron) to within two feet of the flag, and holed the putt. The game was looking easy.

The third was then a short par four, a blind hole from the tee. I stood at the top of the slope and watched Cotton's drive arch past me in a graceful parabola, seeming to hang in the air for a long time before it descended and ran on to the green. There was an air of inevitability about it. The ball was quite a long way from the hole, and Cotton's first putt was feeble, as if to remind us that he was human after all. But he holed the seven-footer securely for his birdie.

The fourth was 460 yards, a testing par five in those days, for it was into the slight breeze. To most of the field, it was out of reach in two that day. Cotton needed a 3-wood for his second, but he was on the green with it; indeed, his putt hung agonizingly on the edge of the hole for a three.

The fifth was 451 yards. Cotton's drive rolled to within three feet of me without any movement from me, as if I had reeled it in on a string. He flighted a 3-iron through the breeze to the edge of the green, and his delicate little chip over the fast-running turf stopped within six inches of the hole.

The wind was assisting him at the short sixth, and he needed no more than his spade mashie to get the ball on to the green beside me, although the tee was almost 200 yards away. As Cotton came to the green, I saw him turn and wave to someone perched up on the hill known as the Maiden, which commanded a fine view over this section of the course. It was a most unusual gesture for him, particularly when he was in the midst of this purple patch of perfect golf.

I looked to see who was the object of his attention, and realized that it was Harry Vardon, who on each day of the championship made his way to this point on the arm of his old friend Arthur Brown and watched the players go past. And each time Cotton came to the green on the sixth, he gave a wave to the two staunch well-wishers above him.

We had started out with a big gallery, but it grew larger all the time as the news raced round the course that Cotton was building upon his first-round 67 and opening a still wider gap upon the field. There were no leader boards around the course to tell the spectators the position of his nearest pursuers, but the feeling that we were in the presence of golfing history grew stronger and stronger as the round progressed.

The crisis came at the eighth. It is nowadays a par four, but it was then a par three, aptly named Hades. Perhaps Henry came off his ball just a little, or perhaps the light breeze gusted a little at the vital moment: from where I stood beside the green, it was difficult to tell. His ball just failed to clear the huge bunker on the right of the green and plugged horribly into the face of it. I surveyed it dismally and did not go to meet my man with the information, feeling that the messenger who brought ill news might like an ancient Roman be summarily despatched.

Bunkers in the thirties were not so immaculately manicured as they are on modern courses, the idea being that the terrain at a seaside links should remain as natural as possible. The bunkers at Sandwich had been sand dunes, of course, and there was a tussock of coarse seaside grass not far in front of Cotton's scarcely visible ball. Butler and he surveyed it; with me standing beside them, feeling as guilty as if I had placed the ball there myself. It looked like the end of the dream.

I could scarcely bear to watch as Cotton struggled to take his stance. He had to take a foothold over a foot below the ball. It was plugged so badly that it looked very doubtful that he could move it very far. If he did not get it out, the probability was that the ball would roll back into the deep footmark he had had to make in the soft sand, or would even hit his person, with the resulting penalty. The crowd gathered ghoulishly around the bunker in a vast horseshoe behind him: there is always a bizarre satisfaction in seeing how the gods of golf can humble even the greatest of its practitioners.

Cotton could not, of course, take a practice swing in the bunker. That meant that the violence of his strike brought an even greater gasp from the spectators than would have been the case had they been prepared. He took a full, slow backswing, then lashed hard into the wall of sand beneath his ball, so fiercely that one feared for a moment for his wrists.

There was such an explosion of sand that I did not immediately see the ball. Then, unbelievably, it appeared at the pinnacle of the cloud of sand, dropping softly on to the green amidst it, rolling slowly towards the hole. Cotton brushed sand from his hair, his face, his neck and his clothing; he tried for a moment to pretend this was no more than a routine shot, then permitted himself a broad smile of relief at Butler and me. The applause rose in a crescendo as he climbed from the bunker and stamped the sand from his shoes. The crisis was past.

The ball had run right across the green, but he almost holed the putt for his three. It was his only dropped shot of this memorable round, but he confessed in retrospect that it felt like a birdie after he had seen where his ball was lying in that bunker. Ten minutes later, he had parred the ninth hole, to be out in 33.

He used a mashie niblick (7-iron) for his second at both the next two holes, getting tremendous backspin on the second of these, played over a ridge of dunes at the old eleventh. It left him a nine-foot putt, which he rolled confidently into the centre of the hole for another birdie.

Cotton kept attacking throughout the back nine, when many would have been safeguarding a good score and a lead in the Open. At the twelfth, he ignored the dog-leg and drove long and straight for the green. It was a glorious hit, but it was gathered in by the big bunker short of the green, leaving him an awkward shot from near the face. He flew it out high and two-putted for his par. After a drive and 3-iron at the 443-yard thirteenth, he was just off the green at the 'wrong' side, but a deft downhill chip to three feet saved his four.

From there on, his finish was awesome. At the 520-yard fourteenth, he was home in two with a 3-wood, and two-putted. The fifteenth was 454 yards, through a tricky cross-wind. After his usual immaculate drive, Cotton came off his 2-iron second just a little, and his ball rolled away into horrid long grass in a hollow to the right of the green. Whilst we all held our breaths he bludgeoned it out with his niblick, then holed a ten-foot putt for a four, to a collective roar of delight.

He finished with three threes, something not achieved before in a championship at Sandwich and, I venture to think, very rarely equalled since. His faithful mashie niblick got him on to the sixteenth green for a two-putt par. At the 423-yard seventeenth, there was a great roar from the crowd around the green as his spade mashie came to rest about eight feet behind the pin.

On the 441-yard eighteenth, he launched a 2-iron second which I thought at the time was the finest I had ever seen. It flew high over the bunker on the right of the green, turned from right to left like a homing pigeon scenting home, and came to rest gently on the green. For such a shot at such a time, I can compare it only with the superb 2-iron with which Tom Watson clinched the 1983 Open at Birkdale.

Crowds had a greater sense of decorum in 1934. They did not shout and whistle; but the applause for Cotton as he made his triumphal progress to the eighteenth green after that splendid shot was as warm and prolonged as the modern greeting now traditionally accorded to great players on the last hole of the Open.

My task as forecaddie was over for the day. I came and stood beside Ernest Butler and Cotton's bag, claiming my peripheral involvement in golfing history. The ball had come to rest only seven feet from the hole; surely at a moment like this, with a crowd like this, the putt would not go in. But Cotton's nerve was supreme, as it had been throughout that memorable day. He stuck out his elbows over his hickory-shafted putter and ran the ball into the middle of the hole, as though such a finish was inevitable.

At last, he could smile his acknowledgement at the crowd and let his elation show. He was round in 65.

It is not easy for modern followers of the game to realize just how revolutionary these rounds of Cotton's were. The lowest score in the Open until 1934 was the 67 in which I had carried for Hagen at Muirfield in 1929. After that, there was only a handful of 68s; scores under 70 were still a great rarity.

Cotton had equalled that Open record on the first day, then beaten it by two shots on the second. His 65, made up entirely of threes and fours, would stand as the lowest individual round until 1977. Even more incredibly, his total of 132 for the first two rounds would be a record for over fifty years.

The 'bogey' score (the score in which a good amateur was thought likely to play the course, 'par' being then an Americanism) for Sandwich in 1934 was 78, against Cotton's 65; and there were plenty of rounds in the championship which did not beat 'bogey'. The course record at Sandwich had stood for twenty years: Cotton had beaten it in each of his three rounds, this time by three shots.

Bernard Darwin as usual was equal to the task of conveying the magnitude of Cotton's achievement. He did it by using the context of the Frenchman who was playing alongside the day's hero: 'Dallemagne, despite one or two loose drives and one or two short putts missed, played splendid golf for his 73. The poor man had averaged fours for two rounds of a course nearly 6,800 yards long, and yet he was twelve strokes behind his partner.'

The course, indeed, was not much shorter than modern ones. The Sandwich course played in the 1934 Open was, as Darwin noted, just under 6,800 yards, only about 100 yards shorter than when the Open was played there in 1985. (Sandy Lyle, the eventual winner in 1985, was joint leader after thirty-six with 139, seven shots more than Cotton.)

And one must remember the tremendous improvement in modern clubs and balls. In pre-war days Cotton and his contemporaries often kept the same ball going through thirty-six holes if they felt they had 'found a good one'. Cotton hit the ball immense distances that day, but he was able to do so only through a complete mastery of the weapons in his armoury. Save for the short holes, he used a driver for every tee-shot, fourteen of them in all. In 1985 at Sandwich, the driver was the exception, with modern pros able to play safe with 3-woods and 1-irons because of the advances in equipment.

I have never seen anyone drive better than Cotton did that day, but he was still playing 3-wood seconds on many occasions, which the modern professionals would never have to do in those conditions. And to produce the score he did, he needed to be as accurate with his 2- and 3-irons as his modern counterparts with 5- and 6-irons.

Finally, his score did not stem from freak putting. He had only twenty-eight putts, but that was because he was so often beside the hole. He holed nothing longer than twelve feet throughout the round; there are only a very few great rounds before or since where that may be said.

The Dunlop 65 golf ball stems, of course, from Cotton's score on that memorable day. The ball has been developed down the years, and no doubt the improvements will go on, but I hope that the name will be preserved for as long as golf is played. That round of Henry Cotton's deserves to be so marked.

It did not merely bring a new dawn for the British game. It ushered in the modern era of golf.

The 1934 Open looked virtually over. Cotton led after two rounds by no fewer than nine shots. Long after he had finished, there was a venomous hailstorm which whitened the greens and made pools on each of them, so that play was held up for a little while until they were swept clear. He scarcely needed such assistance from the elements.

What happened on the last day looks inevitably like anticlimax. In retrospect, it was, I suppose, but Henry Cotton provided us all with a little unwanted excitement.

He had a 72 on the morning round of the third day; after the perfection of his previous golf at Sandwich that week, that does not seem particularly remarkable. But the third day of the championship was almost washed out by violent rain; I spent a night of apprehension, listening to it thudding wildly on the slates above me in my tiny room in the roof of the Admiral Owen.

The seventh green was under water when we got to the

course, but the green staff managed to sweep it away as the storm subsided and the players began only a few minutes late. Cotton was not off until 10.42, so that the majority of the field were ahead of us. The course was playing much longer, with a stiff northwesterly wind. The seventh, which had been a drive and an iron, was completely out of reach for anyone. At the end of Cotton's round, a lady stepped forward and snapped her camera as he attempted a delicate chip. He socketed the ball, kept his composure, and made a five when he could easily have taken six.

We found at lunch that our man had actually increased his lead by one with his 72.

The clubhouse and the surrounding buildings were buzzing as players and spectators made ready for the final round with the talk of Cotton's lead and how it had killed off the excitement. The afternoon could surely be no more than a triumphal progress through his admirers; the crowds made ready to acclaim the long-awaited British champion.

Henry soon altered that view. He had a light lunch. In view of what happened in the afternoon, it is perhaps not surprising that there were stories in the popular Press that he had engaged in premature celebration. That is not true: that was simply not Cotton. He spent the lunch-hour asking people who were congratulating him in advance to leave it until after the final round. He did not indulge in quantities of spaghetti or ice-cream, as some reports said afterwards.

Cotton himself tells it thus:

> I had a light lunch. It would not be telling the truth to say I was not excited, but I did eat enough to sustain

me, and I judged I had timed my arrival on the first tee just right when I got there five minutes before I was due to drive off. The starter, however, to my disappointment, informed me that my time had been delayed fifteen minutes to help the stewards to control the crowds better . . . I went and sat alone in an empty tent by the first tee, while my closer friends talked to my well-wishers, keeping them away from me. Those fifteen minutes dragged by; here I was waiting to see my life's ambition realized and I was powerless to get on with it . . .

This anxiety proved more than my delicate stomach could stand and I had a terrible stomach cramp. I could hardly stand up. I must have looked pretty ill, for I could hear the comments of the crowd on my 'green' colour as I teed up. There was nothing to do but play and get on with it . . .

My own view is that Henry, a naturally nervous man, was thrown completely by the delay – whether or not he emerged from his isolation with stomach pains, he was certainly a mass of nerves, and that in itself meant that he lost the rhythm which is essential to good striking. In the years to come, I would see him control his nerves on many occasions, but he did it always by careful planning. On this occasion, his planning had been thrown awry by changes beyond his control.

I can certainly remember his hands shaking as he took out his driver and waited to get on his way at last at a quarter to three. I hastened off then to my position down the first, but it was quickly apparent that all was not well with my employer. Even from 250 yards away, I could see how he lost balance as he swung at his opening shot. The ball fell a hundred yards shorter than his previous drives, and bounded away into the rough. It seemed that I was about to earn my money as a ball-spotter.

Cotton's long game was dreadful. For thirteen holes he hit scarcely a shot off the middle of the club. The straight ones were short; the better contacts flew to right or left. As he dropped shots, the pressure built, and the silence and disappointment of the great crowd, more eloquent than many words, added steadily to it.

As he reached the sixth green, Cotton looked up to the Maiden, where he had waved to Vardon on the first two days. The great man was not there. At that moment, it seemed like an omen, especially when Cotton missed quite a short putt for a three.

At the seventh, he had three putts from quite close, and ran up another six. But that was an unusual lapse on the green; fortunately, the putting which had served Cotton well throughout the week did not desert him. Time after time, after playing a scruffy hole, he holed out from five or six feet to save a five; it was not good, but the putter saved him from worse.

The first half of the course, with three short holes, was the easier nine. It took Henry forty shots, and it could have been forty-five if his putting had gone the way of the rest of his game. Marking his drives, I had only twice found myself on the fairway. I enquired anxiously but surreptitiously about the progress of his rivals; my old friend Maurice Hart told me that Joe Kirkwood, the American who had been closest to Cotton at lunch, was not doing very much, but the South African Sid Brews, thirteen behind after the morning round, was cutting away at the lead which had seemed impregnable.

The first three holes of the back nine were all relatively

short par fours. In his 65 of the previous day, which suddenly seemed to belong to a different world, Cotton had been on the first two of them with a mashie niblick (7-iron) for his second, and had virtually driven the third of them. Now he took three fives, each time mis-hitting his second shot with the irons that had been so secure for the rest of the week. In effect he had brought himself back a further three or four shots towards his rivals. This was where the ship should have been steadied; instead, it had lurched nearer to capsizing.

The news came now that Brews had finished in a fine 71. Cotton needed 83 to beat him, and at that moment he was seven over fours, with two long holes amidst the six to come.

The crisis came at the thirteenth. He had a horrid lie in a bunker after his second: it looked as if he would be fortunate to get it out and save another five. I think everyone felt that if he left it in the sand the Open would be gone, and gone from such a commanding position that the sufferer might never recover from the experience.

I watched our man take three immense deep breaths before he went into that bunker. Looking down, I saw that my hands, placed together on the top of my umbrella, were shaking, so involved had I become in the drama. The ball was not plugged as severely as the one at the eighth on the previous day, but it was against the face, and the stance was awkward: he could not face the hole. And he was playing badly now, instead of as well as a man ever played.

And the Open hung on this one.

Cotton played the shot beautifully, throwing the ball high in the air before he lost balance, permitting his drawn lips a tiny smile as he saw his ball coming to rest on

Always ready with a quote, always dapper for the cameras! Walter Hagen during his British Open win at Sandwich 1928. Note the introduction of the cine-camera on the right. *Hulton Deutsch Collection*

The first British Ryder Cup team to play in this country, Moortown 1929.
From left to right, back: S. Burns, A. Mitchell, C. A. Whitcombe, F. Robson;
front: E. R. Whitcombe, P. Alliss, G. Duncan (captain), T. H. Cotton;
seated: A. Compston and A. Boomer. Note the golfing attire: only young
Henry Cotton looks remotely like the moderns. *Hulton Deutsch Collection*

The Illustrated
SPORTING &
DRAMATIC
News

SATURDAY, MAY 18, 1929.
No. 2905.—Vol. CXXIII.
Registered for transmission in the United Kingdom.

PRICE ONE SHILLING.
Postage Rate: United Kingdom, 2d. Canada, 1½d.
Elsewhere abroad. 4½d.

Hagen's celebrated left-handed stroke from the wall on the ninth in his final round at Muirfield (see pages 47-8). I am lost in admiration in the foreground! *The Illustrated London News*

Opposite: Cheerful invaders. Gene Sarazen *(left)* and Walter Hagen *(centre)* as the American Ryder Cup team disembark after the Atlantic crossing for the Ryder Cup and the Open, April 1929. *Bob Thomas Sports Photography*

Inset: Bobby Jones studies a putt on his way to completing the historic 'Grand Slam' at Hoylake in June 1930 (see page 63). *The Illustrated London News*

Grace combined with power. Henry Cotton driving from the fourth tee at
Sandwich on the morning of the last day of his Open triumph of 1934. I am
watching anxiously 250 yards down the fairway! *Hulton Deutsch Collection*

Henry and 'Toots' on their wedding day at Caxton Hall, December 1939.
The Illustrated London News

'Be ready to catch this one in the gallery, sir...' Feeding Henry with
ammunition during the stage act (see pages 141-6). *Popperfoto*

Top: Cotton's acceptance speech after his third Open Championship triumph at Muirfield in 1948. Note the presence of 'Toots' as almost the only lady among the seated dignitaries. She was not of course allowed into the clubhouse at Muirfield! *Sport and General Press Agency*

Centre: A bedraggled crew! In Palmer's Open at Birkdale in 1961, play was finally abandoned due to wind and rain. Henry Cotton's umbrella disintegrated at the same moment! I am immediately behind him and the faithful 'Toots', who had followed her man as ever through whatever the elements could throw at her, is under the umbrella behind me. *Bob Thomas Sports Photography*

Right: Cotton never lost his love of the game, even when his triumphs were well behind him. Here we are at Ganton in 1975, when Henry was sixty-eight and I was a spritely sixty-two.

Top: The greatest player from thick rough that I ever saw. Arnold Palmer during his Open win at Royal Birkdale 1961. *Bob Thomas Sports Photography*

Right: 'The tempo of his swing altered not a jot all day, he seemed at peace with himself and the world...' Tony Lema on the first tee at St Andrews, beginning the first round of his Open victory of 1964. *Popperfoto*

the green. It rolled to within seven feet of the hole, when he would have settled for anywhere on the green.

Many years later, we went back to Sandwich to reconstruct this moment as one of 'Henry Cotton's Six Greatest Shots' for a black-and-white television film. Henry had a dozen attempts at reproducing the magic shot: not many of them came out, and none went anywhere near the flag. Eventually the director decided that he would cheat by cutting the film on Henry's bunker shot, whilst I threw the ball gently on to the green and let it trickle towards the flag! It took me at least ten attempts to get the ball within a yard of the flag from my invisible vantagepoint beside the green. This long-delayed postscript made us realize as we came away just how magical that shot had been in 1934, and just how easily the ball could have been left in the sand.

On that far-off day, the young Henry Cotton knocked the putt into the middle of the hole, to a collective roar of relief. The ship had been steadied after all, just when it seemed on the verge of a final, fatal roll. Cotton played the last five in level fours; suddenly, his striking was rock-solid again. He was on the fourteenth green with a drive and an iron. On the fifteenth, a beautiful second gave him the chance of a three; he missed from five feet, but victory was now within his grasp.

He just missed for a two on the sixteenth and a three on the seventeenth, but it mattered not. The eighteenth was the triumphal progress that many had expected the whole round to be. He was bunkered, but played out carefully to twelve feet, knowing that a five was good enough.

His 79 won him the Open in the end by five shots, even though Sid Brews had made up eight on him in that last round. That 79 spoiled a wonderful sequence of scores, but it is evidence again of the towering stature of his first two rounds that Cotton's total of 283 equalled Sarazen's record Open aggregate of two years earlier.

I stayed behind Cotton throughout the closing ceremonies, sharing the euphoria over a British winner after so long. (Eleven years seems to me now quite a short time, but I had been only ten in 1923 when there had last been a British winner of the Open!) Henry had come as he always did dressed ready for golf. He had no jacket, and he had to borrow his friend Henry Longhurst's camel-hair overcoat to wear over his pullover for the presentation.

Henry had a long-standing £10 bet with that other great sporting competitor, Fred Perry, that he would win the Open before Fred won the Wimbledon Singles title. He won the bet: the Open and Wimbledon began on the same day, but it took Perry two weeks to win his Wimbledon crown, against Henry's one!

As soon as he could get away, Cotton took the old claret jug back to the hotel and up to the room of Harry Vardon, who had won that same trophy as long ago as 1896. Vardon had been too ill to make even the short walk to the Maiden on the last day, as Cotton had found from his enquiries in the moment of his victory. As Cotton tells it: 'When I took the old Cup he had won so gloriously on six occasions up to his bedroom, tears came into his eyes, and he could not say a word; nor could I, for I was crying too!'

The public thought of Henry Cotton as intense, even ruthless; and indeed so he was on the golf course. But he was a deeply private man. He was in fact easily moved, but he preferred not to show that to his followers. That he should think first of the old warrior in the hour of his triumph was typical not only of his respect for tradition but of his unvarying feeling for his fellow-golfers. I would witness many such acts in the years which followed, none of them publicized by their instigator.

The flamboyant financial gestures of Walter Hagen were not for Henry Cotton, though he was happy to live in the same luxurious style. Ernest Butler as his caddie was properly rewarded, but he did not receive the cheque for the first prize, as I had done five years previously at Muirfield. But when he died in retirement some years later, and there were no relations to bury this solitary, dignified bachelor, it was Henry Cotton and his wife who went down to his village, paid for his funeral, and mourned him as friends.

Cotton paid me, too, as he had promised, with a bonus on top of the 'few shillings' we had agreed. He looked at me, spruce and tidy as usual among the colourfully ragged attires of the caddie shed. Then he said, 'Well, Hargreaves, you and Butler brought me home in the end, despite myself. I might be able to find some more work for you in the future.' He looked down at me with a small, thoughtful smile.

I thought at the time that it was no more than a parting courtesy, as I prepared to journey north and scratch again for tailoring work in Yorkshire. I would learn in the years to come that Thomas Henry Cotton never said anything he didn't mean.

CHAPTER SEVEN

ASHRIDGE AND LIFE WITH THE COTTONS

AFTER THE 1934 OPEN, HENRY COTTON WENT BACK TO THE Waterloo Club in Brussels and a wonderful reception from the club and the British Ambassador. His humble forecaddie, treasuring the shillings he had earned as if they were the championship gold medal itself, rattled back to Leeds on the London, Midland and Scottish Railway's night train, told the story of the Open to the three uncaring women in the house in Allwoodley, and resumed his search for work.

I was soon employed, but the cloth trade was still precarious; the slow recovery from the great recession was under way, but people were still reluctant to spend more than the minimum on clothes. I was much in demand as a caddie now at Moortown: people were anxious to employ the man who had worked with Hagen and Cotton in two Open Championship triumphs. The caddie-master ensured, of course, that I could not be paid more than the standard rates, a shilling (5p) for one round and one and sixpence (7½p) for thirty-six holes. But I found that my tips at the end of the day were becoming quite handsome.

I was still living at home – mothers discouraged respectable girls from courting lads who had not got secure employment – but after the meagre times of my apprenticeship years I felt relatively affluent. However, I found through the long winter of 1934–5 that I was both bored and depressed; perhaps my contacts with the great moments of golf had unsettled me. I was carrying for some good amateurs and occasionally for professionals at the weekends, but that only reminded me I had rubbed shoulders with greatness. Golf had been good to me so far. I saw no reason why I should not look for further excitement from it.

The spur came when I saw in the golfing press (which I devoured as eagerly as ever, particularly because I now had several friends among the writers) that Lord Rosebery, the driving force behind the newly established course at Ashridge in Hertfordshire, had persuaded Henry Cotton to return from Belgium to become the professional there.

I read it three times, packed my bags, and journeyed south.

Cotton was not yet at Ashridge, but I had not expected him to be. He was seeing out his time at Waterloo, where he had been very happy. Modern readers will need to remember that there was no continuous circuit of tournaments for the best professionals. The biggest and best-run tournament outside the Open was the *News of the World* match-play at Walton Heath.

Apart from newspapers like the *News of the World* and

the *Yorkshire Evening News*, the first private sponsor of a tournament was Sam Ryder, of Ryder Cup fame. In the early thirties, he organized the 'Heath and Heather' tournament at St Albans; the professionals thought it was wonderful, because, in addition to generous prize money for those at the top of the field, all who took part were given £5 and their train fare to St Albans. It guaranteed them a profit on the week!

All the professionals at British clubs were still dependent on their club jobs for their livings. Most of them had contracts which allowed them to be away from the club for only about twenty days in the year. What tournaments there were, including the Open, were organized to finish on a Friday, because the players had to be back at the service of their club members for the weekend. All of them were experts in club repairs: it was the first thing the assistant professional – who was initially not much more than a shop-boy – had to learn.

Most amateurs were still using hickory shafts, though the professionals' shops were beginning to do a brisk trade in the new steel-shafted clubs. The matched set of clubs was still unheard of at most English courses: the idea was to find a driver that suited you, a mashie (5-iron) that you liked, a niblick, and so on. They might all be from different makers, and the shafts were not graded to a standard length. The steel shaft and mass production would soon change all that, but British golf clubs, those traditional bastions of conservatism, resisted for a little longer the notion of matched sets. Henry Cotton would show the way in this, as he did in so many things.

People nowadays forget that Vardon, Braid and Taylor, even Hagen and the young Cotton, assembled their armoury of weapons one by one, working painstakingly on the 'feel' of the club in their hands to see if they were happy with it. The method survives for modern luminaries in the putter: many of them have a dozen or more, switching among them in pursuit of that elusive excellence so crucial to their success. You will often also see in their bags a favourite wedge or 9-iron which is up to forty years old. Most of them, in their contracts with club manufacturers, retain the right to carry up to three clubs of a different make in their bags. *Plus ça change* . . .

I found that Ashridge was a beautiful place. Laid out on National Trust land at Little Gaddesden, the course already looked mature (it dated only from 1932), mainly because of the fine trees which had been preserved in the layout. To my northern eyes, bred on the wild beauty of the moors of Ilkley and the Dales beyond, it looked lush and green, almost sub-tropical in the luxuriance of its growth in that spring of 1935. I had certainly never seen such beautiful turf on a golf course.

I presented my credentials as a caddie for the Secretary's inspection, making sure as usual that I was well dressed and groomed; I had on a starched white shirt and collar and the Sunday suit I had cut with my own hands. The Secretary stood up to welcome me, taking me at first for a visitor wanting to play!

I was soon approved as a caddie; indeed, golf clubs, once they were assured of the honesty and competence of the candidate, had little to lose, for they did not pay him. Caddies were casual workers; if they did not work, they did not eat, unless they had their own resources. I had brought my Post Office book with a few savings as an insurance against adversity, but I did not intend to use it. To do so would have meant that my mother's reservations about the way I was casting myself once again on the

95

golfing waters of life were justified. I sent a postcard home to say that I had found good digs in Berkhamsted and that all was working out well for me. Then I hastened to make that true.

There was plenty of work to be had, for the membership at Ashridge was burgeoning, when other clubs were in difficulties. There was enormous interest because people knew that Henry Cotton, the greatest name in English golf, was coming to the club. People joined it because of that, and the existing membership seemed to play more frequently in anticipation of the great man's arrival. It all meant good business for those sanctioned to caddie. Word of my connection with the great man got round without any talk from me, and I found myself in steady demand.

There were seven large building plots around the estate, the only ones where houses were to be allowed. One of them, I heard, had already been earmarked for Cotton. These acre plots were sold for £150 each; people gasped a little at the expense! There could not have been many more idyllic sites for domestic housing in the whole of Britain.

Through the months which followed, the expectation of Cotton's arrival grew. In the thirties, Little Gaddesden was still a sleepy rural area of narrow lanes and farm horses; the estate which was now partly a golf course had not changed much in centuries. When the great man eventually came, it was rather like one of the 'progresses' of a Tudor monarch through his kingdom.

We heard that Cotton was to take over the Gaddesden Arms in the village, that he would fill it completely with his family and entourage in the months whilst he awaited the completion of his house. This caused a sensation among the locals, even before he arrived. There was dark talk of how the rooms had been inspected by a fierce and mysterious South American lady, who spat fire and set the servants leaping to her commands.

It was said that this exotic creature had Cotton himself under her spell, that the two of them lived together without the benefit of wedlock. Rumour swells quickly into sensation: this witch-like figure became as fearsome in the anticipation as the wicked queen in Disney's *Snow White*, which would shortly be making its own impact on the public imagination.

On one late spring evening, I had finished caddying for the day and was indulging in a little practice of my own behind the beautiful thatched clubhouse. I played to a handicap of four for years, telling those who would listen that if only I could play regularly I would get down to scratch. I was playing a few pitches with a niblick when there was a sound from the narrow driveway to the club as of a tank roaring into battle. It came nearer and nearer, paused when it seemed that it must burst through the trees and roll over me, then ceased abruptly.

I made my way cautiously to the car park to see what monster had announced itself so imperiously. I recognized the vehicle immediately: a red 1929 Mercedes, registration number KJ 1224. Indeed, I only have to close my eyes to see it in my mind's eye today, a low, racy 3.6-litre two-seater cabriolet which would now be worth a fortune on the vintage car market. The slim figure who had just climbed out of it said, 'Hello, Hargreaves. How are you?' for all the world as if he had expected to find me there in that soft spring dusk.

The king had arrived at last.

*　　*　　*

I should say a little about the figure who will dominate the rest of this book, even more thoroughly than he dominated British golf for two decades.

Henry Cotton was the first middle-class golfer to turn professional. In an era when the distinction between professional and amateur was carefully, even jealously, preserved, this meant much more than it would do today. His father had his own engineering business in Cheshire, but his enquiring mind led him into all kinds of projects. Eventually he sold his business in Holmes Chapel and took a post with the London Salt Company. George Cotton moved his family to Dulwich when his sons were boys.

When we journeyed to Scotland to play in the years to come, Henry almost always made a small detour in Cheshire to point out to me the house in Holmes Chapel where he was born. 'Keeps my feet on the ground to remember that!' he would say. It looked a pleasant enough house to me: I think he was just indulging in the romantic nostalgia which his crusty public image did not permit him.

Henry Cotton, sometimes pictured in the popular Press as a humble artisan who had come up through golf, was in fact a public schoolboy. He passed his matriculation examinations at Alleyn's School, and would probably have gone on to university had it not been for a row over the cricket which was his first sporting love. Instead, he decided to become a professional golfer; having taken that decision, he applied himself with characteristic determination to the sport.

In a golf net in the garage next to the house, he pounded the ball far into the night in an effort to perfect his swing. At sixteen, he became an assistant professional to George Oke at Fulwell. Nine months later, he moved to Rye Golf Club as assistant, where he had more opportunities to play, and formed some of the relationships with the university golfers of Oxford and Cambridge which were to last for the rest of his life.

Cyril Tolley, who with Roger Wethered was the finest amateur of an era when there was little to choose between the top amateurs and professionals, was both perceptive and generous about the raw young Henry. He not only gave him sound advice, but played with him frequently, helping to remove the barriers Cotton had set up by his decision to turn professional.

Cotton was at Rye for over two years, so enthusiastic that he often played by moonlight on the close-cropped seaside turf: he always claimed to me that he never lost a ball on these nocturnal outings. Perhaps that experience helped him to become the straightest driver I ever saw in golf.

In March 1926 Tolley's recommendation helped to make Cotton the youngest club professional in the country, at Langley Park Golf Club: he was just nineteen and a quarter. He took examples of his club-making and repairing to show to the committee at his interview. His contract allowed him to charge 4s. (20p) an hour and 2s. 6d. (12½p) per half-hour for lessons. It also permitted him to be away from the club for forty-two days a year to play in professional competitions.

The last clause was the most important one for the young man, as he watched American domination of the Open Championship grow all through his formative golfing years. After seeing Bobby Jones and the great Americans in the Opens of 1926 and 1927, he practised harder than ever, going without lunch on most days and,

99

in his own words, 'hitting thousands of balls every week, often chipping and putting for such a time that it was easier to stay bent than stand up'.

He did not exaggerate. By the time I knew him well, in the late thirties, his body showed the effects of the punishment he had given it to get to the top. The muscles and ribs of his right side were contracted, those on his left were stretched; his spine was bent over to the right and tilted forward. When his new house at Ashridge was completed, he had a bar built in over one of the doors from which he would hang for a few minutes every day.

In November 1928 the twenty-one-year-old Cotton went to America to continue the learning process on the winter circuit there, meeting Walter Hagen and the leading American professionals such as Gene Sarazen, Tommy Armour and Horton Smith. They were friendly and helpful to him, as he in turn would remain throughout his life to young players.

He found that almost all the younger American players had adopted the new steel shafts, still illegal in Britain. It meant that they could practise for as long as they liked, whereas Cotton, like everyone else with hickory shafts, had to guard against fracturing wooden shafts made brittle by too much play.

He also found that he was giving away distance off the tee to the American power play. Taking the advice of Tommy Armour and Sam Snead, he determined to learn to draw the ball, instead of playing the more easily controlled fade he had hitherto employed. He worked hard on the change in the following six months, being much encouraged by his selection for the Ryder Cup team of 1929 at Moortown, where I was able to watch much of his victory in the singles after my match with Hagen had finished so early.

During the following winter, he toured the Argentine with Aubrey Boomer, furthering his education and meeting the lady whom the denizens of Little Gaddesden were now finding so formidable. She booked a month of lessons with him, revealing to him only much later that she had tried first to book with the more famous Boomer!

He went to the Waterloo club in Brussels at the end of 1932. It was partly to improve his earnings – Henry never underestimated his own worth, and professionals were better paid on the Continent than in Britain – and partly to improve his health. It was also partly connected with an event he never publicly acknowledged: the wife of the Argentinian Ambassador newly posted to Brussels was the same small lady who had so attracted him on his visit to her country three years earlier.

The cosmopolitan lifestyle suited Cotton, who spent much of the winter in Monte Carlo and played frequently with the future Edward VIII. Like the Prince of Wales, he developed a liaison with a married lady, though for him it would not have such far-reaching consequences. Fine amateur golfers like Henry Longhurst and Leonard Crawley played with Cotton at Waterloo, and sent him a succession of wealthy pupils.

In July 1933 Walter Hagen, admiring the panache and the lifestyle of the young Cotton, made a spectacular visit to Waterloo for a thirty-six-hole match with the young pretender. He played the course he had never seen before in 69, but was three down at lunch: Cotton had equalled the course record of 66. Hagen eventually lost six and five, and Cotton's friends in the English Press made sure that the defeat was well publicized.

Although they were very different as golfers, off the course Cotton followed the trail that Hagen had blazed. He would often quote to me the advice his father had given him when he set out to make his way in life: 'Always remember that the best is only just good enough for you.' It seemed to me a dictum which might have come straight from the Haig.

Cotton stayed in the best hotels, cultivated a taste for fine wines, made sure that he was immaculately dressed on the course. He was the first British golfer to wear two-tone golf shoes, brown-and-white leather ones, which the makers eventually marketed as Cotton Oxfords. Henry received a one-off payment of £25 for the use of this name, which was used on golf shoes for some forty years. He often bemoaned the fact that he had not negotiated a better deal, but he would not often make such an error in the great years to come!

Many thought him a remote, even a selfish, figure, but he never wavered in his defence of his fellow-professionals. After his victory in the Open at Sandwich in 1934, he walked into the next meeting of the committee of the Professional Golfers' Association. There were raised eyebrows among the grizzled professionals, who asked him politely why he was there. 'I've come to chair the meeting,' said Henry calmly. The jaws dropped; it was so long since a British professional had won the Open that they had forgotten that the current Open Champion, if he was a member of the PGA, became Chairman. Henry Cotton had not forgotten. And the professionals who enjoy such affluence today should breathe a silent prayer of thanks for the earning power he helped to establish for them.

*   *   *

Cotton moved into the Gaddesden Arms as he had planned. The club built a fine professional's shop for him, thatched to match the picturesque clubhouse, and he gave meticulous attention to the fittings within it. His house beside the course was taking shape. A small, dark-haired lady visited the site daily to check on progress; the builders quickly learned that any delay would not be received by her without comment, and it was as well not to offer specious excuses for any lack of progress.

Cotton spoke courteously to me whenever our paths crossed. He used me to caddie for him, though he was at first too busy to play much; I noticed him on a couple of occasions observing my conduct with the other caddies around our shed. He had been at the club for about a fortnight when he came across to me one day after he had spoken to the caddie-master.

'You're a smart chap, Hargreaves,' he said. 'What are you doing working as a caddie?'

It might have been my mother speaking. I did not know quite how to reply; it was not a question I had expected from Cotton. I tried to explain about the hold golf had over me, about the way in which I would rather be making a living from this game than from the trade for which I was trained, even if I could only be on the fringes of it.

He nodded at my stumbling account. I think he understood, for I realized before long that he was the greatest enthusiast for the game I would ever meet in the professional ranks. Hagen played to live, but Cotton lived to play. He played for as long as he could walk, and he would find the decline of his skills through age the hardest cross he had to bear in life.

He questioned me a little more about my background, finding that I had been at Leeds Grammar School, that I

103

knew about the making and care of clothes, that I knew, as he would say only later, how to conduct myself in any company. Then he said rather abruptly, 'Madam needs a caddie, Hargreaves. She won't have any rag, tag and bobtail who sleep under the hedges at night. Do you want the job?'

At first I scarcely knew whom he meant by 'Madam'. Then I realized it must be the mysterious Latin termagant who was installed with him at the Gaddesden Arms: the virago I had watched from a respectful distance at Sandwich in 1934, organizing the formidable figure of Henry Cotton as he ended the American domination of the Open; the spitfire with the ungovernable temper, about whom I daily heard more startling tales. It would surely be rash to the point of stupidity to volunteer for service with her.

'Yes, Mr Cotton. I'd like that,' I said.

I have mentioned that Henry Cotton was the first middle-class golfer to join the professional ranks, setting up for himself a series of social barricades by his decision. My own case was far less important, but in its own way equally unique. I was the first and, until modern times, the only middle-class boy who determined to make a living from the fringe activities of golf, mainly caddying.

There were times in the cheerful and unpredictable world of the tournament caddies when I thought it politic to conceal my grammar school background. I enjoyed that rumbustious and nomadic world, though I was glad to feel that security as well as excitement was now at hand. I suppose I was what would now be called a 'drop-out', though at the time I was conscious of nothing but my overwhelming interest in golf and golfers.

For a while, I kept up my normal caddying attachment

to the club, dropping any other commission instantly whenever Madam decided she would play golf. It was not always at Ashridge: I got used to travelling about the South of England beside the chauffeur in the front seat of a Rolls-Royce or Madam's Minerva.

The lady for whom I carried had certainly a fierce exterior and a natural air of command. I was careful not to offend, but I found her perfectly fair: she expected me to do my job assiduously, but she was appreciative when I did. I was absurdly pleased when she told me as we left one of the plushest clubs in the Home Counties, 'Hargreaves, I can take you anywhere.'

I dare say I should not have been so gratified, but you must remember that those were very different times. And I was beginning to like my formidable employer.

When Cotton's house was almost complete, he sought me out one day and said, 'Madam seems to be well pleased with you, Hargreaves.' He never called her by any other title in speaking to me over the next forty years, just as he never called me by my first name. It took me some months to realize that he could not call her 'Mrs Cotton' because they were not married. By the time they were, the 'Madam' had become a habit, and it stuck.

I said I was pleased that she found my work satisfactory. I think Henry was probing for a reaction from me to her, but I had more sense than to offer him one. 'You can come and work for us full-time, if you want to,' he said at length. He never lost his northern directness, despite his polished manners and society connections. 'I seem to be in need of a valet and a butler, now that we have this big house. You can have a go at both, if you like.'

So it was settled as quickly as that, the post which was to shape the rest of my life. I kept my digs in

Berkhamsted, but I spent most of my working hours in or around Cotton's magnificent new house, Shangri-La. The land of perpetual youth: it was to prove a cruelly ironic name in the last years of his life, when he was irritable and depressed by the miseries of old age. But that was far in the future. Henry was delighted with his new residence.

And so was 'Toots'. The name was given by Henry to the lady of the house because of her diminutive stature. And because her real name was too much of a mouthful for anyone. Señora Isabel-Maria Estanguet de Moss had left her husband for good to be with Henry. They would be fiercely loyal to each other and steadily in love for over fifty years. They had plenty of rows – the domestic context was the only one in which I ever saw Cotton lose his temper – but no-one who saw them ever doubted their affection for each other.

Toots (I should never have dared to call her that to her face, and I apologize to your shade even now, dear Madam, but print demands the shorthand!) came from one of the richest of all Argentinian families. Her step-father was reputed to own an *estancia* covering a greater area than the whole of England; her income from the Argentine Meat Company meant that at one time in those pre-war days she was paying three quarters of her income in tax, half of it in Argentina and half of it in Britain.

She was used to money, to comfortable living, and to servants. Life at Shangri-La reflected that. She and Cotton had separate bedrooms, even after they were married. It meant little, except that like royalty she was used to space and her own apartments. One wall of her large room was completely lined with wardrobes, from floor to ceiling. The large middle section contained dresses and costumes. The lower one was filled with

106

shoes, the higher one with hats, without which ladies rarely appeared in the thirties. Clothes were not put away at random, but in a predetermined order, so that the hats and shoes which had been bought to go with particular outfits were found immediately above and below them.

Her control did not cease at the doors of the house. Whenever she or Henry went out in the car, it had to be cleaned on their return, before the chauffeur went to bed. There was no skimping the task: Toots often went round the car with white gloves the next morning to demonstrate that fact.

The large heated greenhouse at Shangri-La was kept busy. Toots never wore any flowers that were not white. In spring Beckford, the gardener, produced a succession of double white camellias. I had to take the chosen one to Madam for her inspection as she prepared herself for the world. She inspected it from every angle; if there was the slightest imperfection or decay upon it, it was rejected. She never wore roses, though there were often vases of them around the house. In summer and winter Beckford had to produce white orchids for her corsage, which I carried in for the same rigorous inspection as the camellias had undergone.

She knew the house and its environs in every detail, as Beckford and I learned to our cost. One morning when she was out and Henry was teaching, I helped Beckford to move a conifer no more than a foot from the original position she had determined for it when she planned the garden. He stood back with satisfaction when we had finished and smoothed the ground around the new planting. 'She'll never notice that!' he said with satisfaction.

He was called in the next morning. We returned the tree carefully to its original position in the afternoon.

Toots naturally felt the cold in English springs and autumns, and I became something of a boilerman. I had to light the three boilers in the open-ended practice sheds which Henry had set up near his shop. If there was any chill in the air, Madam sent me down to the basement of the house to light and stoke the domestic boiler, often rapping on the central heating pipes a few moments later to make sure that I was there.

I continued to caddie for her whenever she played golf. She was a competent single-figure player, but never more than that. Much to her delight and Henry's surprise, she won the Austrian Ladies' Open in 1937. For many months afterwards, visitors to the house congratulated her, often ignoring Henry's greater and more recent triumphs: 1937 was perhaps the greatest of all his years. 'She was lucky!' he would say with feeling; but he took care not to say it too often when she was within earshot.

On one celebrated occasion, he arrived home on his own from golf at Gleneagles. 'Has Madam stopped off to see friends?' I asked; they were so nearly inseparable that her non-arrival was something of an event.

'No, Madam has not. Madam has merely been her normal silly self!' he said with feeling. It transpired that she had slapped his face in public over some peccadillo on the dance floor. But Henry was at the station to meet her with the Mercedes when she arrived the next day, and their laughter with each other at dinner that night was even louder than usual.

Toots was a devout Roman Catholic, and converted Henry to her faith. They attended Sunday-morning mass in Berkhamsted every week without fail. Even when we toured later with the music-hall act, Mass and Communion on Sunday mornings were invariably a priority.

Ironically enough, when Toots regularized the position by marrying Henry, they were refused Communion by the priest in Berkhamsted, on the grounds that she was a divorced woman.

That divorce was obtained in Latvia, of all places, in June 1939. Henry had been informed that if there was a war, his beloved Toots could well be interned in the Isle of Man as an alien, unless she was married to a British citizen. She was persuaded to undertake the divorce she had always resisted, and became Mrs Cotton after a quiet ceremony at Westminster Registry Office in December 1939.

The more I saw of her, the more I liked her. She was fiery, as everyone said, with Henry as much as anyone. She never quite settled in England; she found it difficult to come to terms with English reserve and the nuances of our society. But she never did anyone a bad turn in her life. And she was kindness itself to me whenever I needed help.

Life with the Cottons was sweet in those years at Ashridge. A German cook, Anna, and two Austrian housemaids lived in the house. Charlie Philbrick, who had been an assistant in the pro's shop before Cotton came, was taken on as chauffeur; I got to know him very well, for in the years to come we spent many hours in the car, waiting for our employer outside places such as the Dorchester and the Savoy.

I learned my business as a valet quickly. Cotton, with his monogrammed silk shirts and his cashmere woollens, was a naturally elegant figure, but I set out to make the most of him. His shoes were always immaculate, but I never used shoe polish: when he was not wearing plus-fours, that would have marked his trouser bottoms. I had noticed the immaculate shoes in the shop window of an old-fashioned cobbler in Godalming, and gone in to learn the secret of the shine. It was Simoniz car wax, which I used on his golf shoes for over twenty years.

His suits were from the West End tailors Hawes and Curtis, his sweaters from Izod (who made some lines exclusively for Cotton and the Prince of Wales!), his shoes from Lotus. I pressed his clothes meticulously and laid them out ready for him, after consulting him about what he needed for the morrow. I used to say, 'There goes the best-dressed man in Britain,' when he set out for the day.

Whenever we went anywhere to stay, I carried Madam's jewel-case. I would hand it to the hotel receptionist to be put in the safe. I was given £2 to put in the hall porter's hand. Nothing more would come if the service was not good, but the news of that first tip usually ran quickly round the hotel.

It was one of the rare occasions when I saw Cotton with money – usually, like royalty, he did not deal in cash. Everything was done by cheque. Henry had a highly developed commercial sense, despite his wife's wealth. He never admitted it, but I think he felt it a point of honour to earn enough himself to support their luxurious lifestyle.

When club professionals were giving lessons for three or four shillings (their prices were usually controlled by their club committees), Cotton charged £5 for a lesson and £10 for a round. These prices showed just how far he had moved on in the decade since he had been giving lessons for 4s. an hour at Langley Park. The increase owed nothing to the modern curse of inflation: prices through the thirties remained generally static. Because of his Open titles and his pre-eminent reputation, he had a steady stream of customers. His friend Leonard Crawley, who became golf correspondent of the *Daily Telegraph*, acted almost as an unofficial agent for him, and there was no shortage of customers.

He enjoyed teaching talented players, but he had an infallible way of dealing with duffers. 'Just go away and practise what I've taught you. Come back when you've absorbed it and feel ready for another lesson,' he would say breezily as he waved them off. Of course, they never did feel they'd absorbed it well enough to be inspected again by the great man.

His teaching system was interesting. He almost invariably taught three people together in the morning. After their tuition, they would be served an excellent lunch at Shangri-La (which annoyed the club committee, who felt they should have eaten in the clubhouse). In the afternoon, they would play a four-ball around the course. This was not two against two, but three individual matches against Cotton, with each playing his own ball against the master. As he usually had a £10 bet on each match, and rarely lost, it made for a lucrative day. The players would be served with drinks at the house before they left. Bruce Thorpe, Cotton's assistant, would bring the accounts over from the pro's shop, and I would take them in for settlement before they left.

'Always make sure you get their money, Hargreaves, no matter how rich they are!' Henry would say to me. He carried the maxim into his dealings with golf clubs which invited him to play exhibition matches. Ten years earlier Harry Vardon, the greatest name in British golf, had been appearing sometimes for as little as £10. For a single, Cotton now expected £300, for a four-ball £200. He made sure the cheques were cashed in advance: 'If it's raining, they might take very little at the gate!' he said.

He had numerous sources of income. Having had to wear a left-hand glove because of an infection in his thumb and an excess of practising, he made a virtue of necessity, ensuring that when his name was given to the glove he received two shillings on every one sold for the rest of his career. He was happy for Dunlop to perpetuate the memory of his 65 at Sandwich by naming a ball after it, but he made sure, even in the midst of the euphoria, that they paid for it: it cost Dunlop £5,000!

At about this time Cotton took over from J. H. Taylor as golf correspondent of the *News of the World*. In those days the paper paid its top writers for life, so that Taylor went on drawing an income long after he had ceased to work for it, as Cotton in his turn did many years later.

Henry never did anything by halves. His professional's shop at Ashridge was the finest I have ever seen, before or since. He modelled it on Harrods' displays. It had illuminated showcases, with 1,200 golf balls and some of the first gleaming sets of matched Wilson clubs on display. It had an impeccably tiled floor, lightly polished cream-and-brown woodwork, and seats covered with zebra hide. All second-hand clubs taken in part exchange were sent to a shop in London for sale: Henry would not sully his immaculate shop with used goods!

He earned only £100 a year at Ashridge, and that was paid by Lord Rosebery; but this suited him. He had negotiated only with Lord Rosebery, and his contract allowed him to go off whenever he chose. The committee and the mass of the members at Ashridge did not like him, and I can understand why. He hardly ever played with the members, and spent much of his time away from the club – as well as his tournaments and other commitments, he and Toots normally spent the worst months of the winter in Monte Carlo.

He had come on his own terms, and he was not prepared to compromise. The club got the kudos and interest which derived from their employment of the Open Champion, excellent practice sheds, and a professional's shop which was like an Aladdin's cave, but not much more. Henry would have said that that was all they should have expected.

Through all his commercial considerations and enterprises, Cotton kept his eye on his golfing standards. He worked hard on his fitness. It was at this time that he began to carry a squash ball in his pocket, squeezing it whenever he had a spare moment during the day to maintain the finger strength he always believed was vital to good hand action in the golf swing. I spent many hours at the opposite end of a cross-cut saw from him, sawing vigorously at the thousands of logs he cut to strengthen his wrists and hands. I was fit and in the prime of life, but he could leave me exhausted, and took a delight in doing so.

He took a pride in going to every tournament ready to play, in every sense. My job was to see that he was immaculately turned out; his was to be sure that he was in a physical condition to give of his best. He always made a point of thanking the people who had organized the tournament before he left, however well or badly he had done in it. 'It's easy when you've won. The real challenge only comes when you've lost,' he would say to me as we roared away in the red Mercedes.

In all the years I was with him, I never saw him lose his temper on a golf course. He had learned early that there was no future in that; like Bobby Jones, he had fought successfully to control a rebellious temperament. But he never spoke to anyone whilst he was playing serious golf. He used to say, 'Hargreaves, neither you nor I would dream of bursting into the office of the managing director of a company without an appointment and beginning to chat with him. Well, the golf course is my office, the place where I work: I can't work properly if I have interruptions to contend with.'

His intensity meant that his fans did not see the sense of humour which was so evident in private. I saw it when he journeyed home with me in the car, or when he entertained his friends, or most particularly when he was alone with Toots. Their repartee with each other was always a delight.

The Cottons never had more than four people to dinner whilst they were at Shangri-La. I always laid the table and served the meal. The talk would go on into the night, and Henry was a delightful and witty host. Almost their nearest neighbour, with a house on one of the other plots beside the course, was the famous Russian-born pianist Benno Moiseiwitsch. I can remember him playing Chopin on the Cottons' Bechstein grand, with the lights turned low in the drawing room, while the clock crept past midnight and I listened entranced behind the kitchen door.

But always it was golf which was Cotton's ultimate hobby. Anyone who had played with him was always welcome. He was never a snob, and never pompous. He did not mix socially with most of his fellow-professionals, but he was always prepared to help them and never bore a grudge. He wrote hundreds of letters of recommendation for young pros on the way up: 'If I can get them started, it's then up to them to see how far they can go,' he said.

*　　*　　*

He had not been very long at Ashridge when he came to me in the May of 1937. 'We're off to Carnoustie, Hargreaves. I've taken a house up there for the Open – we'll be better away from hotels and well-wishers.'

My pulses quickened as always for the Open, as I knew my employer's did. He put his head around the door of his shop with an afterthought: 'Better bring your woollies, and pack mine, ready for the frozen North. It might be a bit wild up there, but we'll give it a go.'

It was. And we did.

CHAPTER EIGHT

THE OPEN OF 1937

THERE WERE OTHER IMPORTANT GOLFING MATTERS TO BE dealt with before we could move up to Carnoustie for the Open.

The Americans brought to the Ryder Cup of 1937 what was generally agreed to be their strongest team of all until that time. That view was borne out when the match took place at Southport and Ainsdale on 29 and 30 June. On the first day, Cotton, coming to the course straight from church on the feast of Saints Peter and Paul, lost in the top foursomes with Alf Padgham, the current Open Champion. Padgham was not in his best form, and on the second day he lost his singles by eight and seven.

The British team was routed, winning only two and halving one of the eight singles. All matches were still over thirty-six holes, and the United States beat Great Britain by eight matches to four; it was the first time the

Cup had been won by a visiting team. Home hopes had been high, despite the strength of the Americans, for Henry Cotton was in the Great Britain team for the first time since the victory of 1929 at Moortown. (He had not been eligible for selection during his attachment to Waterloo.)

Henry won his singles by five and three; standing beside him, I thought him the only man in the British team who was striking the ball with the same consistent solidity as the opposition. Our only other winner was the young Dai Rees, who beat Byron Nelson by three and one.

The British public was disappointed, as well as suitably awed by the skills of the transatlantic invasion. Even Leonard Crawley, when he had failed to qualify for the Open at Carnoustie, went back to London and wrote for his newspaper that we need not look outside the ranks of the American Ryder Cup team for a winner of our 1937 Open.

Walter Hagen was the non-playing captain of the American team, and we had quite a chat about old triumphs. He was most complimentary about the golfing skills of my new employer. 'You know how to pick 'em, Sonny,' he said, 'but then you always did!' He was still calling me Sonny after the war, when I was well into middle age.

Because the Haig was not playing in that Ryder Cup, he probably relaxed a little too much in the bar, because he made a famous blunder in his gracious speech as winning captain. He said how nice it was for his team to win for the first time on 'home soil'. There was a buzz of puzzlement around his audience, but Walter recovered with his usual panache, by pointing out that as he had won the British Open four times he was bound to feel at home here. He got prolonged applause, characteristically turning his gaffe into a strength.

In retrospect, the Ryder Cup seems to my rather partial eyes little more than a prelude to the great individual events of Carnoustie.

In taking a house for his entourage at Carnoustie, as in so many other things, Cotton was setting a trend which is followed by many of the modern great players. 'In a hotel, even the best hotel, I cannot relax as completely as I need to do to give of my best on the golf course,' he said. It was true enough. He was the greatest name in British golf; in a hotel it was impossible for him to get away from his well-wishers without seeming churlish.

So the family – Toots had two daughters from her previous marriage – and servants moved into a large house within a mile of the course. It was to be my job, as butler and valet, to keep the temporary household running smoothly and send the great man out to tackle the rest of the golfing world in the best possible condition.

Henry was used to having me at his side during play, and wanted to use me on the course, on the grounds that he wanted everything as normal as possible in the contest to come. I pointed out that I could not be everywhere at once, and neither he nor Madam would be pleased if they returned to a house which was not running smoothly as their base of operations. Toots, who would as usual walk every yard of the way with Henry, would not be there to supervise either his meals or his wardrobe.

There was, in the end, no difficulty. Ernest Butler, that dignified and knowledgeable man who had caddied through the 1934 triumph at his native Sandwich, made the long journey north for the last of his great assignments.

He and I always got on well, meeting in a pub in the evenings to exchange ideas, swap golfing stories, and decide how best to support our man the next day. Ernest was my idea of what a caddie should be, low-key and taciturn, never volunteering an opinion unless it was sought, but a fount of golfing wisdom when his player felt he needed it.

When I saw the size of some of the bags that week, I was quite glad not to be carrying. There was still no restriction on the number of clubs, and some players loaded as many as twenty-six on the backs of their unfortunate carriers! When a maximum number of clubs was set a little while later, there was a strong lobby that it should be ten, rather than the fourteen which eventually prevailed. Ten has always seemed to me about the right number, encouraging golfers to learn versatility in their skills, as well as cutting down on the interminable time it takes some modern pros to make decisions; but I fear the club manufacturers are now too powerful a lobby for the matter ever to be reconsidered.

I would forecaddie as I had done before at Sandwich and elsewhere, marking our man's ball on a course which was not only long and demanding but had thick and punishing rough. Lots of balls were lost during that wild week in early July, but our golfer was never in danger of losing one. The chief reason for that was not my sharp eyes but Cotton's own high skill, in conditions which could scarcely have been more demanding.

Because Cotton made his usual preparations for the Open, it has sometimes been reported that this was his first visit to Carnoustie: it was a mistake he helped to perpetuate by a slip in one of his books. In fact he could well have won there in 1931, when he was joint leader after two rounds. He blamed his friend Eliot Cockel, publisher of *Golf Illustrated*, for his collapse then, because he came up on the overnight train from London to advise Cotton to play cautiously in the third round. This did not ring true, for Henry Cotton was never anything but his own man on a golf course, and he admitted privately to me that it was no more than an excuse for his own poor striking on the last day.

We had journeyed to Carnoustie in May, not only for him to refresh his memory of the course, but so that he could study the changes which had been introduced to make it a severe test of the world's best golfers for the Open of 1937.

The Ryder Cup finished on Wednesday, 30 June. We journeyed straight north for the Open practice days: this was a hectic fortnight in the lives of the top golfers. Henry practised assiduously on the Friday and Saturday – I noted as always the contrast to my days with Walter Hagen – and pronounced himself 'reasonably satisfied' with his game. It was as far as he was ever prepared to go: translated into layman's language, it meant he was in high form.

As always, he did not plan much work on the Sunday, choosing to husband his resources for the demanding week ahead, with its six stroke-play rounds over five days. That was just as well, for a terrific rainstorm emptied itself over Carnoustie on that day, driving players from the course and filling its hollows with water. But in the evening the sun shone and the wind blew from the southwest: by Monday morning, all was well for the qualifying rounds, apart from the odd residual puddle here and there.

The biggest crowd of the day followed us round the

Burnside course, where we were for the first day of qualifying. Bernard Darwin reported that Cotton did not seem particularly happy with his putting, but he played steadily enough for a 72. We had more rain overnight; on the Tuesday a morning of drizzle threatened floods. But the water was swept away and the links recovered. Cotton, on the much more demanding championship course, had a 73, to qualify comfortably enough with 145; the American, Horton Smith, led the qualifiers with a fine 138, but all these scores would now be discarded. The preliminaries were over.

Wednesday, 7 July, the first day of the championship proper, was bright and fine, with no more than a pleasant breeze from the sea in the morning. Cotton was away after some of the big American names, and the encouraging news filtered back that they were making a few mistakes. From my vantagepoint down the course, coming close to my man only occasionally before I moved away to receive his next shot, I could not tell whether he had even registered the news from other parts of the course. He had wrapped himself as usual in his blanket of concentration.

But his game was in good order. He began with four fours; then, at the fifth, he found a bunker from the tee, and it cost him a stroke. When he found another with his drive at the sixth, I stood beside his ball knowing that the first crisis of the Championship threatened. His ball was against the face of the bunker, but he got it out well, and then played a glorious long iron to the green to save his par. He found a greenside bunker at the short eighth, but laid the ball stone dead. He found his fourth bunker in five holes at the ninth – two of them had been from

121

unlucky bounces, but I had more sense than to inform him of that when he arrived – and it turned a difficult four into a five.

On the way home, he struck his long shots far and accurately, as the 7,000-yard course demanded. He struck his putts well on the fast greens, but no long ones dropped. Had he holed more, he would have transformed a respectable score into an excellent one; but at least he missed no short ones. He was round in 74, and Bernard Darwin was able to report the next day his view that 'This round represented a fine piece of fighting and leaves him in a reasonable position.'

That position was improved in the afternoon, when the wind freshened and scoring grew more difficult. There was one brilliant afternoon round, from the American Ed Dudley, who produced the day's best round of 70 in the day's most demanding conditions. It left Cotton four shots behind, in joint tenth position after the first day.

The morning of the second day provided ideal golfing conditions, and the scoring became hotter. Dudley tacked a 74 on to his 70, but it was the dashing and brilliant Reg Whitcombe, going for everything and bringing most things off, who seized the lead by adding a 70 to his first-day 72.

We were out just after lunch, with the wind once again freshening to a stiff breeze, making both club selection and striking more difficult than in the morning. We had a crowd with us which stretched from tee to green; I had repeatedly to push through them to make sure I had the best view of Cotton's drives in order to mark where they came to rest. There was a great weight of expectation upon him, but he was used to that by now.

His game was not quite as solid as in the first round, and he had to hole a series of saving putts to be out in 36.

122

But on the second nine he struck the ball majestically, splitting the fairways with his drives and making my job very easy. He struck a superb 4-iron second to within six feet of the fifteenth hole, but the putt lipped out. Then he was bunkered at the sixteenth and took a five at the last; what had seemed a possible 69 became a 72. Bernard Darwin mirrored my feelings that night exactly when he wrote: 'The pace is so terrific, the standard so high, that even these venial slips may be terribly important when Friday evening comes.'

At the end of this second day Cotton lay joint fourth, alongside the holder of the title, Alf Padgham, and the 1933 champion, the American Densmore Shute. This distinguished trio were four shots behind Reg Whitcombe. The leader's brother, Charles, occupied second place jointly with Ed Dudley. The scene was set for a titanic struggle on the last day.

It was at this point that the weather chose to add its own contribution to the excitement. I woke several times during the night to the sound of rain drumming on the roof. We rose on Friday, 9 July, to a sodden world and a course in danger of submersion. I did not believe that Carnoustie could take so much rain and remain playable, but I reckoned without the free-draining terrain and seaside turf of this great links.

It was to be a close thing, especially when the deluge became even fiercer after lunch, but we just about got through. Nowadays play would undoubtedly be suspended in such conditions, at least for part of the day, but the drive to complete came from the British professionals themselves, who knew they must be back in their club shops on the Saturday to attend to the needs of their members!

The Olympian Cotton was, of course, above such

considerations. He viewed the downpour with distaste but philosophically, coolly calculating the odds as to whether it increased or decreased his chances of success.

He looked at his three acolytes as we prepared to make our way to the first tee through the relentless rain: the small but resolute figure of Toots, covered from head to foot in waterproofs, determined as ever to walk every inch of the way with her man; the ageing but calm figure of Ernest Butler, affecting a stolid indifference to whatever the elements could provide as he shouldered the bag for two rounds on this awful day; myself in cap and mack and a pair of his discarded golf shoes, my dapper exterior soon to be washed away by the rain. 'My team should give me the edge over the rest!' he said with a small, determined smile.

Reg Whitcombe was off early, playing throughout the morning in a steady drizzle, but with the greens neither so waterlogged nor so trodden as they became for the later starters. He was round in 74 while Cotton was still struggling on the course; with his overnight lead of four strokes, he was going to take some catching in these circumstances. Cotton set out to hang on; there was always the possibility of an afternoon collapse from the leader in this appalling weather.

Even in these conditions, he contrived to look almost elegant; certainly in appearance at least he was the most serene player on the course, accepting whatever fortune chose to fling at him with an unruffled demeanour. I never saw his short game better than in those last two rounds at Carnoustie, and he saved himself time after time in this third round with the most delicate pitching and chipping from lies where each shot threw up a little spurt of water from the sodden grass.

124

And one by one, his rivals began to drop away. Padgham had a 76 and Dudley a 78; both were six behind the leader as he went into the last round. Densmore Shute, the most feared American, hung in alongside Cotton until the last two holes of his morning round. Then he dropped a stroke at the seventeenth and underclubbed the eighteenth, so that his ball dropped into the Barry Burn. Those strokes dropped when he had almost completed the task of his morning round were Shute's death knell; he had an 80 in the afternoon and disappeared from contention.

Those last two holes were crucial for Cotton. He had taken five at the fifteenth and four at the sixteenth, hooking iron shots in each case. We came to the demanding seventeenth wondering if he would drop too far behind the leader to make an afternoon challenge. He answered us with the finish of a champion. He made his four at the seventeenth, where many were dropping shots. Then he hit a vast drive to the home hole, which made it easy for him to clear the swollen Barry Burn. But he did more than that, dropping a splendidly controlled iron to within eight feet of the hole and then running the putt into the very centre of the hole. There was a great cheer from the sodden ranks of the faithful, standing six-deep around the green.

That priceless three gave him a 72: he had made up a stroke on Reg Whitcombe, reducing his lead to three. We looked at the skies, wondering if the contest could be completed that day if they did not relent.

For a little while, they did. At midday the rain stopped, after pouring continuously for twelve hours. But, as throughout that day, there was little wind to move the clouds on. We dried out as well as we could, and hoped.

Then, at just after one, having rested and refreshed itself, the rain returned, with such a ferocious deluge that it seemed that all must be abandoned for the day.

Bernard Darwin wrote in *Country Life:*

> The hollow in which the first green lies was getting more and more waterlogged as the day wore on, and the hole was being re-cut nearer and nearer to the slope on one side. There was an awful moment about lunch-time when a distinguished player refused to start on the justifiable ground that the first hole was unplayable . . . Something was done, play went on, but all through the afternoon the authorities were on tenterhooks, and if anybody had lodged a formal appeal against the conditions I think it must have been upheld.

Reg Whitcombe began his final round with three fours, but then met the full force of the torrential rain as it returned. As he drove at the seventh, the slimy wet leather of his driver grip slid right through his grasp and the club flew from his hands. His ball scarcely cleared the front of the tee and the hole cost him a six. Yet he carried on heroically through the worst of the weather and produced a 76.

Whitcombe had been out early, and the news filtered back to us on the course. It meant that Cotton would need another 72 to head him – we could not see anyone else getting near. That score did not seem on in these conditions. I looked at Cotton when the news was relayed to him, but he remained inscrutable; he told me later that he had scarcely registered Whitcombe's score, so preoccupied was he with his own game.

In truth, he had need to be, for he was not, in the first half of his round, striking the ball as well as he would have liked. Ernest Butler, with his hair plastered in wet ribbons and water running off his face, secreted a towel jealously in the intimate recesses of his clothing to keep it dry, producing it briefly beneath his umbrella to wipe a grip and then returning it hastily whence it had come. He and I would laugh almost hysterically as we recollected that process over our beers in the evening; but at the time there was not a smile in sight.

The ball was stopping dead as it pitched on the fairways, and landing on the greens with a splash of water which was visible from afar. It was difficult to be certain of two-putting from any distance, and almost no-one was holing the long putts which might have rescued a score in more normal circumstances. Seventy-two did not seem on; I wondered privately whether the 73 which would give us a tie was possible.

If Cotton's striking was not always supreme in that last round, he gave what Darwin called 'an exhibition of boiling down three shots into two which has in such momentous circumstances never been surpassed.' He got his four like this with a chip and putt at the first. At the second he grasped the jewel of a birdie by holing from over twenty feet after a rifle-straight iron to the heart of the green. He chipped and putted for his pars at each of the next three holes, preferring to be straight and a little short rather than risk the waterlogged bunkers if they seemed to threaten.

He hit two glorious wooden shots at the long sixth, almost carrying to a green which no-one reached on that sodden afternoon. With another deft chip and putt, he had his four. He made his only slip to drop a shot at the seventh, but he chipped dead at the ninth to be out in 35.

Suddenly, it was on. We scarcely dared to acknowledge it to ourselves, but we all knew it. 'Keep it going, Cotton,' said Toots, affording him the luxury of an encouraging smile.

After the thirteenth, he was two under fours; in those conditions, even the crowd who had followed him so faithfully and cheered home each putt found it difficult to believe. He chipped and putted again at the fourteenth for his par, then missed his only short putt on the fifteenth. The crowd buzzed, but we all knew what he had to do now. Two fours and a five over Carnoustie's remorseless finishing holes would see him home in front of Whitcombe.

As if the elements had a proper sense of drama, the fury of the downpour now redoubled; so fierce was the deluge over those closing holes that the drops were bouncing up from the already sodden ground. Cotton responded with an equally dramatic counter-thrust; he hit a fine tee shot and gave himself the insulation of an invaluable three at the sixteenth.

Some say that he was lucky at the seventeenth, but I was beside the green and know that he was not. The ball hit the umbrella of a spectator, but was thrown left and short of the green; without the deflection, it would have been pin-high on the green, not wide of it, as some claimed. The deflection mattered little, for Cotton chipped and putted as securely as he had done throughout the day to make his four.

That meant that he could make a six at the eighteenth and still be one ahead of Whitcombe. But as the leaders were not out last, there were still many players behind him, and there was always the nagging doubt that someone at the rear of the field might be doing great things which had not yet been reported.

Cotton hit a good drive at the 525-yard eighteenth, far enough to ensure that he did not need to play short of the Barry Burn, as he would have done had he felt there was a risk of disappearing into its watery depths. With out-of-bounds on the left, he played a 2-iron as far right of the green as he dared, aiming at the bunker at its right edge. His ball found it unerringly, and there came the final moment of drama as he surveyed the muddy ball in the sand compacted with water.

There was out-of-bounds on his line behind the green, so he chose not to use his broad-soled sandblaster, lest it bounced off the sodden sand and flew off the front edge of the club. Instead, he took his pitching niblick and played out deliberately short of the hole, taking two putts for his five.

Toots threw her arms high in the air, then seized the top of Henry's strong right arm and would not let it go. Ernest Butler's exhausted face was suffused with the pure joy of a child's. With a Yorkshireman's sense of economy, I retrieved the sodden cap I had flung high above the crowd when the last putt went in. That crowd was still cheering long after I had it back.

Only Henry Cotton, golfing realist, said through his smiles of acknowledgement, 'Not all the scores are in yet. We'll have to wait to be certain.'

The rest of them went back to the house, and I waited. I spent several shillings in telephone calls from a kiosk behind the clubhouse, relaying the scores back to base as the players came in; Shute with an 80; Bobby Locke with a 79; my old employer, Walter Hagen, waving wearily but cheerfully to me as he came off the green, with an 81.

Only when I told Henry that his last challenger, Reg Whitcombe's brother Charles, had come in four strokes behind him, did Henry finally accept that nothing could go wrong and he had won.

This is generally accepted as the greatest of Cotton's Opens, though all have their advocates. The first ended ten years of American dominance. The last is, I think, my own favourite, since it was achieved when many thought his greatness had passed from him. But there is no doubt that the 1937 triumph at Carnoustie was achieved against the strongest of fields, with the full might of the victorious American Ryder Cup team as well as the best European players ranged against him.

He had reduced his score in each succeeding round, producing two scores which no-one had believed possible during that fearful final-day deluge. Cotton thought himself that his last round here was perhaps his greatest ever, surpassing his 65 at Sandwich because of the manner and circumstances in which it was achieved.

There was a bizarre and hilarious sequel, one of those occurrences with which Toots constantly put life into perspective for Henry. On the way home they journeyed to Calcot Park, near Reading, to play in a mixed foursomes tournament which Toots had claimed as the price of her unswerving allegiance in the Carnoustie monsoon.

She gave her usual stern injunction to Henry not to leave her in the rough with his drives from the tee – a reasonable enough injunction, since she was not physically strong enough to hack the ball out of heather or long grass. But even Open champions are human, and Henry, perhaps relaxing a little after his efforts in Scotland,

130

strayed into the rough with his drive on about the eighth hole.

I was caddying as usual on these occasions for Madam, and we had walked ahead in the approved foursomes manner to be ready to play the second shot. It wasn't a bad lie, and I suggested a 7-iron. To my surprise, she took up her stance not facing the hole, but back towards the tee. Then she thrashed the ball with all her might back towards Henry, to the astonishment of the crowd. 'That will teach you to put me in the rough, Cotton!' she said decisively.

It is sometimes quoted as an example of Toots's high temper, but it was at least partly an example of the humorous horseplay in which the two of them often engaged. Henry certainly seemed amused rather than outraged. It was a story he told many times at dinner parties in the years which followed, for it immediately provoked the listeners to ask how he reacted.

In fact he looked hard towards her across the fairway for a moment, and then took his brassie from the bag. Then he rifled the ball long and low at the distant flagstick. It rolled to within three feet of the stick amidst applause from a rather bewildered audience. Toots walked to the green, holed the putt as if this was the most natural four in the world, and made her dignified way to the next tee for her tee-shot. I thought it a considerable performance by both parties.

Enthusiasm for golf had never run higher in Britain than in the weeks after Cotton's second victory, and the *News of the World*, through its famous sporting editor, Sir Emsley Carr, decided to keep this interest on the boil. In Carnoustie's storm the American Ryder Cup players had trailed in disconsolately behind Cotton, not disgraced –

131

there were seven Americans in the first fourteen – but put firmly in their places. There were some mutterings about British conditions having defeated them, though I knew that Henry too had rarely played in such vile weather. Nor was he physically a strong man: it was the high level of his golfing technique which had produced that marvellous final round. The *News of the World* set up a challenge match between Cotton and whomever the US Ryder Cup team might nominate as their resprepresentative. The match was to be over seventy-two holes at Walton Heath, with £500 put up for the winner.

The Americans chose Densmore Shute. He was both an appropriate choice and a formidable opponent. He had been Open Champion four years earlier at St Andrews. He was the reigning American PGA Champion, with a reputation as a good match-player.

Shute played well at Walton Heath, but over two days and seventy-two holes he was worn down by a man at the height of his powers and in wonderful form. The Old Course at Walton Heath is quite exposed and a lovely test of golf. In bright July weather, the pleasant breeze seemed zephyr-like after the wildness of the links at Carnoustie. Cotton had successive rounds of 71, 70 and 69, and Shute was vanquished by six and five.

We returned to Shangri-La in the September of 1937 well satisfied. Henry Cotton had won the British, German and Czechoslovakian Open titles and had defeated top Americans in Ryder Cup and challenge matches. It was always a good place to come back to. The house and gardens were established now, looking very beautiful as the red Mercedes roared in through the gates.

Hitler was making noises about the need for 'living space' for the German people, leaning hard on his native

Austria, where Toots had lately won her Ladies' Open title. A few Jews were beginning to transfer their residence to Britain, and bringing strange tales with them. But surely no-one could take that posturing puppet we saw on the newsreels seriously?

We put aside thoughts of the war which that alarmist Winston Churchill kept saying we should have to fight. There would be new golfing tasks for Henry in 1938. One of them would be a bizarre sort of challenge, which no-one could have anticipated.

CHAPTER NINE

A HEROIC ROUND AND A VENTURE INTO THE THEATRE

1938 WAS A STRANGE YEAR. FOR GOLFERS LIFE WENT ON AS usual, but the country lurched nearer to war. At the end of September, we all thought it had come, until Chamberlain flew home from Munich with his famous piece of paper and promised 'Peace for our time'.

We went back to Sandwich, scene of Henry's triumph four years earlier, for the Open. Henry struck the ball well, but the putts did not drop. After opening rounds of 74 and 73, he was seven shots behind the leaders. 'We shall have to go some tomorrow, Hargreaves,' he said as he sipped the single glass of claret he allowed himself with his dinner.

But he awoke to a day when survival seemed the limit of ambitions. People on the seafront near the house were being blown over, were clinging to lamp standards to stay upright in the gale. It was probably the wildest day on which golf has ever been played in an Open. Today play

134

would certainly be suspended in similar conditions: the safety of the spectators alone would demand that.

Henry Longhurst wrote in the *Evening Standard:*

> The wind was the strongest I have ever known in the Open Championship, and conditions must have resembled those at Muirfield in 1929, when Walter Hagen's final rounds of 75 were reckoned some of the finest golf ever played. On the way out against the full force of the wind it was like playing in the days of the guttie ball . . .
>
> I have just made a tour of the wreckage of the great exhibition tent, and a very pathetic sight it is. For a long time the main poles stayed up and it looked like a great eight-masted schooner in full sail, but a short time ago it sunk with all hands, and now traders are busy among the debris trying to find the remnants of their stock.

I well remember the destruction of that tent. Bits of debris whirled about the course. You would see a sheet of something hurtling towards you on the breeze and hope to goodness that it was brown paper, rather than something more substantial. At lunch-time, we sought what shelter we could and looked in amazement at the litter of steel-shafted clubs which lay twisted and broken in the wreckage.

There were some bizarre feats and some awful disasters in that wind. Alf Padgham drove the green at the 384-yard eleventh and holed the putt for a two. But one player had a fourteen at the twelfth. At the long fourteenth, Cotton's old friend and mentor Cyril Tolley followed a good drive with a fiercely struck 1-iron. The ball cleared the canal by some distance, then blew back into it. Tolley, one of the strongest strikers in the field – he was famous for twice driving the 370-yard eighteenth at St Andrews in a 1927 competition – had two 86s on that wild Friday.

Poor Ernest Butler could scarcely stand with Cotton's clubs, but he knew every inch of his home course; he marched in the lee of the dunes whenever he could, back arched against the wind, often edging along laterally against its force. From my vantagepoints down the fairways, he looked like an elderly crab as he made his sideways progress. I crouched low in whatever shelter I could find, sometimes on all fours, always watching like a hawk for Cotton's drive, for the wind could whip the ball away as though it was on a rope.

Cotton, leaning hard on the wind at times to retain his balance, produced the finest golf of that awful day. He looked exhausted when he came in at lunch with a fine 77. It took him a long time to summon the concentration to check his battered card before he signed it.

Watching his face grey with the effort, I doubted whether he would be able to keep such golf going in the afternoon. But as he and everyone else tired, he did not just hang on, but played better and better. He thought at the end of his career that this round was 'very nearly the best of my life'. It was certainly the most heroic, for the conditions were even more demanding than in his great 71 of the previous year. John Jacobs, now perhaps our most famous teacher, saw that round as a boy of thirteen and recalls its magic even today: 'Henry didn't win, but for umpteen years after that every time I played golf I was Henry Cotton.' Even today, the dwindling number of people who saw that round raise it instantly when they meet me.

Many of the par fours became demanding fives for the world's best players. Cotton took whatever advantage he could when the wind favoured him. He drove the 370-yard second and holed the putt for his two. He drove the 384-yard eleventh, as Padgham had done, and two-putted for his three. These were magnificent shots, even with the gale behind them, for they demanded great accuracy of striking with a driver over that distance.

He hit the ball remarkably straight throughout the round, even when one would have said that the vagaries of that brutal wind made it impossible. More often than not, I was on the fairway when I crouched beside his ball to mark it. But Reg Whitcombe had already posted his score of 78, and Cotton needed a well-nigh impossible 71 to tie. He was three under fours on the thirteenth tee, and for a moment the impossible seemed to beckon. But the last two holes were out of reach in two, and the dream faded.

He was home in a magnificent 74, the best last round by three clear strokes; but Reg Whitcombe's 78 carried him to the title he had just lost to Cotton in the previous year. The champion was two in front of James Adams and three in front of Henry Cotton: they were the only players to beat 300 for the four rounds. It was the last time that British players occupied the first three places in the Open.

Henry played several successful challenge matches after the Open, but he turned down the most lucrative offer for interesting reasons. Bobby Locke, who was to be the biggest name in British golf for some years after the war, had only recently turned professional after an impressive amateur career. His South African manager, Len Oates, now tried to set up a match with Cotton for 1,000 dollars.

137

It was a big sum, but Cotton refused. When Oates persisted, he replied that he would play Locke only if there were no advance publicity, which would mean few spectators and minimum newspaper coverage. Not surprisingly, the match did not take place.

Cotton's reasons for this intrigued me. 'It took me ten years of hard work to get to the top as a professional. I'm not having someone who's done nothing yet climbing on my back. Denny Shute was the American PGA Champion and had lots of titles behind him when I played him in that *News of the World* challenge last year. Let Locke win a few like that, or an Open, then I'll play him.'

There was a loyalty to his fellow-professionals in this: he would have played any established British player for a smaller prize than was offered for Locke, but he was not prepared to give an unproven player the publicity and stature which a big match against him would bring, win or lose. Locke was not a member of the British PGA, and was trying to get round the restrictive five-year eligibility rule. Henry supported his association; he was always serious when people talked money, but money was not everything.

Cotton and Reg Whitcombe in fact played a seventy-two-hole four-ball match against the two South Africans, Locke and Sid Brews, at Walton Heath. There was quite a lot of needle between Locke and Cotton, not only because Cotton had turned down the singles match, but because Locke had won the Irish Open by a stroke from Cotton in the previous week at Portmarnock. Cotton had been fragile on the greens in the last nine, whilst Locke had holed putt after putt, provoking the unwise comment from Cotton that he was 'a lucky young fellow'.

After Cotton arrived late on the tee, Locke deliberately

took an inordinate length of time in studying his putts during the round: the annoyance of the opposition was in no way diminished when he then proceeded to hole almost all of them. Locke was round in 63, putting the South Africans two up after the first thirty-six holes. He was berated by the newspapers for his funereal pace, but that only increased his determination for the second day.

Cotton and Whitcombe, however, played fine golf in the morning, and were one up at lunch after a pulsating third round, setting up a great finale to the contest. Locke went out in 32 in the afternoon, regaining the lead for the South Africans at the crucial stage of the match. He was holing everything on the greens again, and taking an unconcealed delight in doing so.

Then, at the twelfth, Cotton played perhaps the most famous shot of his distinguished career. When played down the dog-legged fairway, the hole measures 391 yards. Whitcombe duly followed the South Africans to the middle of that fairway. Henry looked at the skies, then towards the invisible green. The wind was behind him. He addressed the ball on the line of the green. There was a little buzz of excitement from the spectators behind the tee as they noticed this change of alignment.

Cotton was noted as the longest and straightest driver of his generation. Like Nicklaus who followed him, he always appeared to have power in reserve. This time even I, who had taught myself to be professionally phlegmatic, gasped at the ferocity of the contact as he sent the ball away.

It seemed to be in the air longer than any other ball I had seen, soaring far out over the heather. There was a great cheer from those behind us, then a ragged, astonished shout from the thinner lines of spectators near the distant green. Peter Dobereiner in his biography of Cotton estimates that the ball carried 350 yards through the air. I was there, and I think in this case enchantment has lent a little distance! Even with the brisk following wind, I do not think any man could have carried the ball as far as that with the equipment then available. I estimated the carry at the time to be something just over three hundred yards.

But Cotton as usual had calculated his risks carefully: his partner was safely on the fairway if his venture failed, and the ground near the green was clear of heather, though dotted with scrub and small trees. He would need luck with his bounce, even if he got the drive right and carried the heather, but his partner should be safe for the four if he failed.

He got his luck. The ball cleared the heather, bounced erratically but helpfully through the bushes, and rolled to the edge of the green. It was a shot which only an idiot or a great golfer would have contemplated. And Henry was no idiot. Even Locke, who had no reason for sycophancy, declared then and reiterated at the end of his career that this was the greatest drive he had ever seen.

It was the *tour de force* which won the match. Cotton made the birdie his drive demanded and squared the match. The British champions swept on to a two and one victory. Years afterwards, when we went back to include this episode in the television reconstruction of 'Henry Cotton's Six Greatest Shots', which I mentioned in an earlier chapter, the trees near the green had grown and the drive was totally impossible, however favourable the conditions. It took me several attempts even to throw the ball far enough from the shelter of those trees to reach the edge of the green when the director elected to 'cheat' in the recreation of that celebrated shot.

If there was animosity between Cotton and Locke, it did not survive into their mature years. When Locke became a quadruple Open champion in the post-war era, Cotton gave great attention to Bobby's skills in his books and articles. As always, Henry was fascinated by golfing methods, and Locke's repeating hook was one of the most individual approaches ever to win a string of titles.

War clouds did not prevent ventures to the Continent in 1938: Cotton retained his German and Czechoslovakian titles (an ironic double at the time of Munich) and added the Belgian Open.

In the late autumn of that year, my employer came to me and said, 'How do you fancy going on the stage, Hargreaves?'

I was mystified, though I remembered him appearing briefly in a golfing sketch with Leslie Henson, Eddie Gray and Fred Emney a couple of years earlier. This time, it seemed, Charles Tucker, an American impresario living in London, had invited him to put together an act of his own which could be used on stage.

I did not see how it could be done. As usual I underestimated Henry Cotton. 'You won't have to look for golf balls – Madam won't be playing!' he said to me. Then he set about writing a script for himself.

That was where the problems came. It was not until we got into the theatre itself that we realized how carefully he must stick to his prepared words. There was a series of lighting cues, each one of them a phrase in the script he had prepared and given to the management. Unless he delivered the exact words in the correct places, as printed in their copy, the lighting staff could not put on and switch off the lamps as required.

It took several rehearsals before he was word-perfect enough to have the whole thing going slickly. I too, who had never been on a stage in my life, had to learn to step forward and disappear into the background on cue, for my actions also were sometimes triggers for the stage and lighting staff.

I was surprised what an entertaining act Cotton had devised. He walked on with an old hickory-shafted club and a gutty ball and briefly demonstrated their disadvantages, hitting into a net.

Then came the first lighting cue: 'I shall now show you golf in a different light.' The golf clubs, balls, shoes and gloves he used were covered with a fluorescent paint and the lights changed to an eerie ultra-violet, which obscured all but these key points. He took the audience through what was basically a beginner's lesson: the difference was that without a pupil he proceeded by the demonstration of his own skills.

The audiences were fascinated by the display of his expertise. As in so many things, art conceals art, and a good swing looks easy. It was only when the maestro explained what he was doing that the people in the theatre realized just how much control he had over a golf ball, and how much more was involved in the game than simply hitting the ball a long way.

'If you turn your shoulders too soon, the ball will go to the right,' he would say calmly to the microphone. Then, as I teed the ball for him, he would mutter to me, 'I hope to goodness it does!'

Invariably it did, just as when he brought in his shoulders too late it went to the left. I stood watchfully in

142

the darkness. My part was to place a succession of balls on the mat for the demonstration shots, and to hand him a succession of clubs in a pre-arranged order. I wore a sports coat with open pockets, which I had enlarged specially for the act. I had ordinary golf balls in those pockets, to be hit into the net during the demonstration.

My trouser pockets were stuffed with a different kind of ball, created specially for the purpose so that they could not damage anyone they hit. Henry would hit these soft balls into the audience at the end of the act to demonstrate the accuracy of his striking. He would ask for people to stand up in various parts of the theatre, then land a ball neatly into their hands, to roars of appreciation from the surprised audience.

He leavened his script with plenty of humour, and demonstrated that on the subject of golf he was an avid and fascinating talker, full of lively ideas. I had heard it often enough around his dinner table when I was acting as butler, but it was fascinating to see it transferred to this larger context. The act allowed Cotton to demonstrate the showman which he never allowed himself to be on the golf course, and he thoroughly enjoyed it.

I relished my part as straight man, assistant and occasional stooge. Moreover, Henry paid me £5 a show, whereas I had been getting 35s. (£1.75) a week for my multifarious duties at Shangri-La. I naturally remember our show-business foray with great affection!

We appeared for two weeks at the Coliseum, with a bigger billing than Nellie Wallace for the first of them. I remember the audience joining in the strains of her famous 'My old man said follow the van . . .' with much excitement, for it was our cue to be ready in the wings. Florence Desmond was with us in the second week. We

143

met her again forty-eight years later when she appeared with the rest of us to pay homage to Henry on *This Is Your Life* in 1986: she flirted charmingly with the aged Henry – poor Toots was dead by then!

The act lasted about twenty minutes, and the shows were twice nightly. At first Henry nipped round to the Savoy and had dinner between the shows, but he soon found that cleaning off the make-up and reapplying it for the second house was making his skin very sore. So he went for dinner after the second show finished, at around 11.30. When he met friends, he was there until one o'clock or later. Charlie Philbrick and I sat in the car outside the Savoy for hundreds of hours on these and other occasions, our employer being the most gregarious of men when he found himself among friends.

During our second week, Henry said to me, 'We're in for a bit of trouble tonight, Hargreaves.' Brigadier Critchley, a noted amateur golfer with a reputation as a hell-raiser and a considerable following, had hired the first two rows of the stalls. As Henry had given him several thrashings at golf and fairly short shrift in conversation, the rumour around the theatre was that a collective 'raspberry' was in preparation.

If they came to jeer, they stayed to applaud. The act went down better than ever that night, and it was the rows of good-time boys at the front of the stalls who led the response. The rest of the cast, who had assembled nervously in the wings to provide moral support against the threat of the 'bird', were most impressed with Henry's aplomb and the way he worked with the audience to get them on his side.

We toured not only the variety theatres which were then abundant in various parts of the capital but those in the rest of the country as well. Leicester, Nottingham, Bristol, Manchester, Edinburgh, Glasgow: we became part of that travelling show-business world. Except, of course, that Henry made sure that we stayed always in the best hotels. He was paid £10,000 for sixteen weeks: it was more than anyone could make from golf, as even Toots allowed.

We were warned to expect trouble at the Glasgow Empire. In fact, the manager told us that Henry Cotton was a bigger draw than Harry Lauder: certainly the theatre was fully booked four weeks before our arrival. And the Glaswegians loved him, perhaps because they understood his golfing skills better than most. Even the drunks, who barracked traditionally on Friday nights when they had been paid, were silent and appreciative. One of my functions was to take up to the star the piles of autograph books left for signature. There were more of them in Glasgow than anywhere.

We played everywhere to packed houses. Henry enjoyed it. 'I could do sixteen weeks of this every winter,' he said with a gleam in his eye. The preparations were soon in train for another season, but a certain Adolf Hitler disrupted these, as he did so many other plans. Neither of us thought, as we bowed to the packed houses in the winter of 1938–9, that we should have other and more serious concerns in a year's time.

I thought the war had seen the end of the stage act, but in 1953 I got an unexpected summons to rejoin Cotton in the show-business limelight. He had been selected for the new Queen Elizabeth's Command Performance. Not many people realize that there is only one of these in each reign: the subsequent years are Royal Variety Performances, to which the organizers invite the monarch. Cotton

145

was selected by the monarch herself, who had chosen the theme of the British Commonwealth and invited 137 performers.

We rehearsed the old act for two days: it came back surprisingly quickly, and the star's skills seemed undiminished. All he said was, 'Thank God I don't have to show them how to putt!' He ended the act triumphantly by depositing one of the soft balls into the Royal Box, landing it precisely in the hands of his volunteer, the Duke of Edinburgh.

CHAPTER TEN

WAR AND THE AFTERMATH

IN SEPTEMBER 1939 HENRY COTTON CAME BACK TO SHANGRI-La after staying with friends and sought me out immediately. 'Hargreaves, I think you should know that I've decided to volunteer for the RAF. I don't know what—'

'That's all right, Mr Cotton,' I said. 'As a matter of fact, I enlisted myself, ten days ago.'

So our lives were drastically altered, as suddenly and as simply as that. No-one was naive enough this time to think the conflict would be 'over by Christmas', and it was quite clear that for the duration of the war there would be no tournament golf, the régime that had motivated both of our lives.

I had been about to depart for America with Cotton for the Ryder Cup and a prolonged tour when the crisis over Poland deepened and the country moved towards war. I was intensely disappointed at the time, for I had been looking forward to a visit to the United States with a

147

young man's impatience. The thirties was the era of Hollywood at its most extravagant, and the USA, still a week away by sea, was invested with a romance accentuated by distance.

Ten years earlier, Walter Hagen had asked me to accompany him permanently on the burgeoning American golf circuit, but my mother had vetoed that for a sixteen-year-old. Although I had grumbled, I had been secretly a little pleased, for I was not really ready at that age for such an adventure. Now I was eagerly anticipating the voyage and the work in America. We were all set to sail on the *Manhattan* when Hitler intervened.

The events of that war are not the subject of this book. I had seven years in the RAF; Henry Cotton had rather fewer, through no fault of his own.

There were so many volunteers at the outset of the war that there were not enough uniforms or weapons to go round, and we had to wait a few weeks before the system could be expanded to cope with us. We were a little way into the war before Cotton sold the old blood-red supercharged Mercedes Cabriolet, which had carried us so swiftly and noisily to so many venues. He had bought it second-hand in 1929, and driven over 100,000 miles in it. Now it went for £120, and when I saw it driven away I felt for the first time that we were at the end of an era.

I had myself acquired my first car, which I left in one of the garages at Ashridge when I went to the war. When I returned a couple of years later, I had to get rid of it. The garages had been filled to the roofs with thousands of rolls of fine cloth, bought and stored there by a prominent London tailoring firm. If the worst had happened and jackbooted hordes had taken over the country, they would have been well and expensively clothed. Whilst the war effort demanded every ounce of energy and resolution from those living in the capital, some people were making prudent provision against all eventualities . . .

Cotton had won the German Open just before the political situation deteriorated beyond repair. The President of the German Golf Federation was killed in the war, but at the end of 1945 his secretary sent Henry a cheque for his prize winnings of 1939!

Cotton had been in the Officer Training Corps at Alleyn's; he became a probationary pilot officer. He had a civilian flying licence and was expecting to become a fighter pilot in a Spitfire or Hurricane. But there were too few aeroplanes at the outset of the war to cope with the volunteers. He was turned down for flight training on the grounds of age (he was thirty-three at the time). It was the first brutal reminder of the passing years: he had always until now felt himself a young man in a game which was peopled with older men.

He became a catering officer. As he had for ten years been obsessed with the importance of diets, he took what was meant to be a routine job seriously; from what he told me when we met, I have no doubt that he made a thorough nuisance of himself to people who were busy with what they considered more serious concerns. As a humble AC1 who had to suffer the vagaries of a range of military cookhouses, I thoroughly approved of his concern!

Before very long, Henry was moved from Shrewsbury to RAF Halton: we aircraftmen considered it hardly a coincidence that this was no more than a few miles from Ashridge. The impression was confirmed when Toots was appointed librarian to the Officers' Mess at Halton: she even got a petrol allowance! They had been married in

December 1939, and were able to spend much of the time at Shangri-La. There must have been more RAF officers playing at Ashridge during the war than on almost any other course in the kingdom.

To those of us who were being hounded by both the German and the British military machines, this seemed an ideal war for Cotton. But this lethargic existence did not suit a man who had always set himself goals and pursued them relentlessly. When I came back to Ashridge on leave in 1943, I found him very depressed. He felt he was not making his due contribution to the war effort, despite the fact that he was raising very considerable sums by playing exhibition matches with eminent professionals who were too old for military service, such as his friend and adversary Alf Padgham.

His depression was increased when the thatched club-house and his magnificent shop were burned to the ground in 1943. Cotton was at Ashridge at the time, ordered to bed on account of a stomach ulcer that was causing him increasing pain. It did not improve things when it emerged that the cause was not the German incendiaries which had damaged so many British buildings but a local hand, a man who felt he had a grievance against the club.

Toots rallied assistance with characteristic energy during the fire, and they saved quite a few of Cotton's sets of clubs, together with the hoard of new golf balls which were very precious in those war years, when none were being manufactured in Britain. When they went next morning to collect them from the putting green where they had been deposited, they found that all that had been salvaged from the fire had now been stolen.

This disaster seemed to Henry to symbolize his position.

He was making no direct contribution to the winning of the war, and was unable now to earn his living from the game he loved. Worse than that, he felt acutely the loss of the years of his golfing prime to the war. If it seems unworthy that a man should be so concerned with a game when great affairs of state beckon, you must remember that it was the game to which he had devoted himself with a single-minded obsession since he was sixteen years old. He had worked supremely hard for his mastery, and now that mastery was useless.

His depression was increased by his physical condition. When I next returned, he had undergone an operation for his duodenal ulcer after being invalided out of the RAF. He was unable even to play his fund-raising exhibitions for the Red Cross. He played a few holes with Toots, white-faced but determined. For the only time when they played together, I carried his clubs, not hers. It was the only time also when she was not critical of his bad shots. Her sympathetic silence was much more depressing than the high-handed criticism she visited upon him when he was fit.

I did not come out of the RAF until the beginning of 1947. I went to see Cotton to tell him I was getting married. He was living in the Dorchester, in defiant luxury as we entered the years of post-war austerity. He and Toots had installed all their best furniture from Shangri-La in their Dorchester suite. He told me that he had wintered in Monte Carlo, helping to revive the course there after the war, combining his advisory work with a period of convalescence after his operation and two serious illnesses. 'I had forty German prisoners of war working for me, whilst they waited for repatriation,' he said. 'They were easier to manage than you, Hargreaves.'

He was looking forward to resuming serious golf in 1947. Despite his health and what he called his rusty skills, he had won the French Open in 1946 with the lowest four-round total he ever compiled, 269, against the course's scratch rating of 300. He had added a record 65 on the East Course at Wentworth to the record of 65 for the West Course which he already held: he could take me through each shot of it several months later, and I dare say both of our faces lit up at the account.

He told me he was going to be professional at Royal Mid-Surrey. 'Come and work for me again, Hargreaves,' he said. 'We'll be back in harness soon.'

Toots added her invitation, telling me that they would have need of me when they had their own apartment and could 'move out of this place'. She looked round the sumptuous Dorchester suite as though it were a seedy lodging house.

I said resolutely that I was no longer free to indulge my passion for golf as in those carefree pre-war days. I was shortly to be married. We hoped to have a family in due course. I must look to the future: I was a trained tailor, my wife had complementary skills. We hoped to set up and develop our own business. Golf must now be a hobby, not the central element in my life.

I think that at the time I almost convinced myself of it.

I married Ivy, and I have never regretted it. We have been together now for forty-five years. We set up our business, at Buxton in Derbyshire. There was not much money to spare for clothes after the war, but people had not given much attention to their wardrobes since 1939. Not many men were satisfied with the 'demob suits'

152

accorded to them by a grateful nation, and Dior's 'new look' brought much interest to the female market. We did well enough.

But we were fearfully cold in Buxton in the bitter winter of 1947, when every pipe in the shop and our flat froze solid. And, truth to tell, I was bored. I watched Cotton's scores anxiously during the glorious summer which followed that harsh winter.

He had not looked at all well to me when I saw him at the Dorchester. Although he had fought hard to make himself a golfing machine in the thirties, he had never been strong physically, and had always had to husband his resources carefully against the demands of tournaments like the Open. Secretly I wondered if his great days were over. Perhaps, selfishly, I wanted to be convinced that my decision to turn away from golf for my living was justified.

I went as I had always done to the Open, meeting Cotton and many old friends there, most of them for the first time since 1939. It was at Hoylake, and Cotton was joint leader after the first day with a fine 69. I followed him all the way, and felt the old excitement stirring again in my veins, like a returning friend. But on the second morning he looked tired and apprehensive, rather than the confident warrior of old, and he tailed away to a sad 78.

There were other changes to remind us that the years were passing. My programme carried the stern injunction that 'Bicycles must not be brought on to the links.' The old days of boys retained by my Press friends to rush details of the latest happenings from various parts of the course were over. We had moved on a little from the days when I began to attend in 1926, when a handwritten list of the leaders near the tent where the score-cards were

153

returned was the only information about the general picture. But the board with scores near the eighteenth green was still the only attempt at relaying the changing happenings to the public at large.

The gentle Irishman Fred Daly took the title, and Cotton finished joint sixth, only four strokes behind but very tired. 'I'm going to have to build myself up with some decent grub, Hargreaves,' he said as I took my leave. I noted that he had not lost his old preoccupation with diet.

He enquired about the success of my tailoring work and my new wife, listening courteously to my guarded account of our success. Then he looked hard at me with that keen look from beneath his greying eyebrows. 'Come and see me if it doesn't work out. I'm sure Madam could find something for your wife, if she'd like that.'

I spent many of the small hours in the nights of that autumn wondering how Ivy would get on with that formidable female presence.

Cotton went off to America to 'build himself up' and we beavered away at our business. We built up quite a clientele, and it was obvious that we could make a reasonable living, and perhaps more than that. But Ivy could see I was not happy, that I missed the glamour and excitement of my pre-war existence.

By the spring of 1948, she could see that I was chafing in the new harness I had given myself. 'Go and see your Mr Cotton,' she said, in that determined way women have when they have decided to indulge the schoolboy lurking in all men. 'But don't do anything silly.'

I went. By the time I got there, I had forgotten her second command.

CHAPTER ELEVEN

BACK WITH COTTON: THE LAST GREAT TRIUMPH

COTTON LOOKED MUCH FITTER WHEN I WENT TO SEE HIM. HE had been in America for a lengthy visit, believing that the plentiful supplies of food there were necessary to the revival of his health. Whatever the reason, he looked bronzed and at peace with himself, though considerably older than when I had last worked with him on the golf circuit in 1939.

'We've sold Shangri-La,' he said. 'We shall be moving into a posh place in Eaton Square. Winston Churchill wanted it, but we beat him to it.' Henry always seemed to be guying himself and his success when he spoke in private, so that I did not take him very seriously at the time. It was only later that I found there was some truth in the story: Churchill had apparently expressed an interest in the place as his London base, but the Cottons had taken over the lease before that interest could be taken further. It was the ultimate symbol of the arrival

155

of the golf professional among the élite of the land.

Some, including his biographer, have castigated Henry Cotton as 'a terrific snob, who loved a lord almost as dearly as he revered a millionaire.' I can only record that I knew him for over fifty years, working closely with him for some fifteen of them, and was never treated other than courteously and fairly. I have recounted that he never called me anything other than 'Hargreaves' and I never responded with anything other than 'Mr Cotton'. Still less would I ever have thought of addressing his formidable wife as anything other than 'Madam'.

But I was as happy with those arrangements as they were. They helped to define my working situation, and it was helpful to me that neither party thought of stepping outside them. Things would no doubt be different now, but remember that we first met in 1929, when I was sixteen years old. We never broke our rules, even when he was gravely ill and I spoke to him in a Paris hospital, as I shall presently relate.

Henry was accused of courting titles and money, and it is true that he supported a lavish life-style from his golfing activities – more lavish than anyone other than Walter Hagen had been able to do before him – but he chose his friends carefully, even among the rich. He would part rich fools from their money adeptly, but he never sought their company. And, in the main, it was peers and royalty who courted him, rather than the reverse.

Above all, he always had time for golfers, especially his fellow-professionals. Not only did he much improve their lot by improving his own, but he gave young professionals hours of tuition and advice, without ever charging them a penny. Over the years, he wrote thousands of letters on behalf of young men who were making their way in the game.

And he took a genuine delight in teaching, in improving the game of even mediocre players. Even Peter Dobereiner, who wrote the biography quoted above, conceded that 'Cotton's snobbery was strictly an off-course condition. When he had a golf club in his hand he was a Samaritan anxious to help the needy.'

I never knew the Cottons to be other than absolutely fair with any employee, however humble. When I now turned up out of the blue they were glad to see me, and concerned to know how I had been getting on. It says much for the kind of trust there was between us that I had agreed within minutes to work for them again, and that they had agreed to take on Ivy, whom they had never seen, to work with me in their new apartment at 74 Eaton Square.

They knew me, and they accepted my assurances as to her capabilities as a cook. Neither party needed anything on paper to seal the agreement.

The Cottons entertained only small groups of friends in the sumptuous apartment at Eaton Square, but they entertained them lavishly. The Sheraton dining table seated up to twelve, and on occasions it took me two hours to lay it fully for dinner.

We used lace tablecloths in elaborate designs. We had different-coloured heat-proof covers to go underneath these, and sometimes Toots, who as always ran her eagle eye over all our preparations, would decide when all was laid that she would after all prefer a different colour.

There was normally just one red wine with the meal, almost invariably a fine claret. For the rest, there was

157

champagne and the most comprehensive selection of liqueurs that I have ever seen. The table glittered with silver and exquisite cut glass. Every wine glass had the initials 'H.C.' engraved upon its side.

The whole set-up at Eaton Square was the visible announcement and guarantee that the professional golfer had established himself and could hold his own with the best in the land. The furnishings were mostly antiques, gathered with care in the salerooms of the capital, which were suddenly full of fine pieces as death duties ensured the break-up of great houses after the war.

But there were reminders still that golf was the centre of this world. It was golf that had drawn me back in the spring of 1948, and it was not long before we were making the familiar reconnaissance and preparation for the Open Championship. When Cotton told me that he had booked a house in Muirfield in preparation for the contest, I felt at last that the war was really over and my world was returning to normal.

The weather on the practice days was quite difficult, with raw winds beneath lowering skies. As usual, Cotton spent the Saturday practising on the course, but relaxed and gathered his energies on the Sunday for the first day of qualifying. When we went out to do battle on Monday morning, I felt I had turned the clock back twenty years, to when I had come here as little more than a boy and carried for Walter Hagen as he took the championship.

Things had not changed very much. Women were still not allowed in the clubhouse, much to the disgust of Mrs Cotton. If you look closely at the photographs of the presentations at the end of the championship, you will see the diminutive figure of Toots standing on the steward's balcony, outside the sacred precincts of the clubhouse itself.

The course had been set up just as Cotton would have wanted it, with lots of rough and narrow fairways: he would miss just one in the course of the week. There were gleams of sun peeping through the clouds which banked black and menacing over the Forth, and a light northerly breeze, as there had been for the qualifying back in 1929.

It seemed too much to hope now that Cotton would take away the title at the end of the week as Hagen had done all those years ago. I had looked apprehensively at the husky American figure of Frank Stranahan, the Amateur Champion that year, as he compiled a 67 in practice at Muirfield, and wondered how many other young golfers would be challenging for the title in this new post-war era. Cotton was forty-one, and many people said his great days were gone.

But on the first day of qualifying, he began his answer. He played a characteristically calm and attractive 69, beautifully compiled and without any real alarms. At Archers' Wood, the eighth hole, there was no chance of driving into the rough and making the hole easier, as Hagen had done so memorably, for new plantings prevented it. Nevertheless, Cotton got a three there, laying a marvellous long iron shot dead by the pin. I was glad to see that he looked comfortable with his putting: that was always a good guide to his potential on these occasions. His 69 led the scores at Muirfield.

Tuesday dawned grey, cold and windy, but Cotton was out at the end of the field, and the day had improved somewhat by then. At Gullane he played with supreme confidence, compiling a round with only one five in it. This was at the fifteenth, when he was long ago sure that he had qualified. He took three from the edge of the green, and followed this with three putts at the short sixteenth. They were his only lapses: he was round in 69 again, and led the qualifiers by two shots. We were back in business.

When the championship proper began on Wednesday, 30 June, conditions were ideal for golf, with a light westerly breeze which died all day to a complete calm in the evening. There had been no rain during the night, and the greens, never easy at Muirfield because of the myriad subtle borrows, got drier and faster as the day went by.

Roberto de Vicenzo, the popular Argentinian, holed his second shot with a 2-iron for an albatross on the 513-yard seventeenth and came in with a 70. He and Fred Daly, the defending champion, had finished joint second behind Cotton in the qualifying, so they were plainly men in form; Daly produced a sound and workmanlike 72 to stay right in the hunt.

Sam King, whose father had been a charcoal burner in the Weald of Kent, had been deprived even more than Cotton of the great years of his career – he was born in 1910. This gentle, equable man, a great lover of wild life and highly esteemed by Cotton, led the championship from the moment he completed the first nine holes in a splendid 33. He was back in 36, so that at the end of the first day he led the field with the fine Belgian player Flory van Donck and little Charlie Ward from Little Aston. All three of them were round in 69.

Whilst the news of the progress of the rest of the field filtered back to us, our man was having his own problems. Cotton began by driving into a bunker, to a great sigh of disappointment from his vast gallery behind the tee.

Thereafter his play to the greens on the first nine was as fine as I ever saw it. But he had changed a month or so earlier to a new putting style, with his weight on his right foot and the ball well back in his stance. It had worked well throughout the qualifying rounds, but now suddenly it looked awkward and ill-conceived.

He three-putted the fifth, the seventh and the eighth; as always on these occasions, it seemed from the bursts of applause that everyone on the course around us was holing putts. He was out in 37, and when he had a five at the tenth it seemed that the writing was on the wall.

It was then, when his round seemed to be slipping away, that Cotton showed himself as the great champion he was. He made a fine three at the eleventh: Toots took his putter and kissed it as he came back to his bag. From that moment on I can recall not a single slip, on the green or anywhere else. Despite starting back with that five, he was home in 34. What had looked at one time like a 75 or a 76 was transformed to a 71.

At the end of that first day, he was lying joint sixth, alongside the pre-tournament favourite, the Australian Norman von Nida. Just about right for the first round, said I and the rest of his supporters over our beer that evening. Well up with the leaders without being at the front too early.

Back in the house, Cotton himself would admit only to gloom over the test match result: Bradman's Australians had just beaten England by 409 runs.

King George VI came to watch the second day of the Open on 1 July. He could not have chosen a better occasion.

It was a perfect golfing day, with high white clouds

161

moving slowly across a blue sky in the gentlest of breezes. From the start, a welter of good scores came in, so that I wondered unworthily whether our ageing master golfer would be able to match them and stay with the pace.

Charlie Ward threatened to put a real gap between himself and the rest of the field. He was out in 36, then started back 4, 3, 4, 2. With a 68 beckoning to add to his opening 69, he had trouble with bunkers, and took two sixes at the last two holes to come in with a 72. It would leave him still in second place at the end of the day, but those sixes destroyed his championship.

Cotton was formally presented to the King before he set out – a curious procedure for one who had played many rounds with the monarch in the past. He started as one inspired, with an immense drive, an easy iron to eight feet, and a confident putt for a three. At the third, he chipped short and took a five, but it was the only blemish on his round. In fact, it was the only five in it.

He played the next six holes in three under fours. At the par five ninth, he placed his drive precisely into the spot which we had agreed in practice was the right one, then hit a magnificent second to within fifteen feet of the hole. When he holed the putt for his eagle, he was out in 33. Those who had come to see the monarch watching Cotton were now riveted by the golf.

He started back with three fours, then put in a burst of three threes in four holes: that at the fifteenth came when he holed a long, curling putt which was afterwards measured at forty-seven feet. That one fell in when it appeared to have ceased moving; I think the roar of delight from the crowd was the biggest I had ever heard on a golf course.

He ended with two faultless fours, the one on the

eighteenth being almost a three, for his putt rimmed the hole, but this time stayed out. His round of 66 was made up of that single five on the third, ten fours, and seven threes. I think it was the nearest to perfection I ever saw him play, for he was never in real difficulty throughout. (One cannot really compare this with the heroic rounds in rain and wind at Carnoustie in 1937 and Sandwich in 1938, for the conditions were so different.)

My memory does not play me tricks, for Bernard Darwin wrote of Cotton's 66 at Muirfield: 'Neither I nor anyone else has ever seen him play better, more calmly, or more confidently.' Incidentally, it is often written that the King followed every stroke of that round; in fact he watched the last nine holes only, for the impartiality expected of the monarch dictated that he should see others before he turned to his old friend.

At the end of this glorious day, Cotton's 137 led by four shots from Ward and King. Arthur Lees and Flory van Donck were five behind, with the formidable quartet of Padgham, Daly, von Nida and de Vicenzo gathered a further shot behind. With two rounds to be played on the final Friday, it was not all over yet, despite Percy Boomer's assurances to us that 'Only one man can beat Henry and that's Henry himself.'

Those words from Cotton's friend were in my mind even as I awoke on the last morning of the championship. In the middle of the third round, it seemed as if they were about to come true.

He was the second man to start, and I had never seen such crowds assembled by the first tee so early in the day. He was playing with his friend and nearest rival, Sam King – that of course was merely the luck of the draw in

163

those days, as was his early starting time. Henry began with three fours and a three, with no hint of an alarm. I relaxed, feeling that after this ideal start he might go even further away from the field.

Then disaster came from nowhere. Without playing a really poor stroke at any of them, he dropped a shot at each of the next five holes. The only perceptible difference was that he became suddenly fallible with the putter which had served him so well on the previous day. He was out in 39. King, despite a six out of nothing at the ninth, had gained a shot on him.

Worse was to come. From outside Cotton's ball on the tenth green, King holed a very long putt, whereupon Cotton took three from no great distance. When another five followed at the eleventh, King was suddenly level with the man many had thought was uncatchable.

It was at this point, with his temperament under the severest of examinations, that Cotton showed his mettle. When he missed his putt on the eleventh, his wife called him something unprintable when he came back to her. He said, with a tired smile, 'I'm only human, Toots.' Her look announced that even that might shortly be in question.

Madam's unique mixture of exhortation, cajoling and rebuke often seemed to work for the man she understood so well. He produced a three and a two at the next two holes; the crisis had not found him wanting. From that point on, he played soundly, if not with the serene mastery of the previous day, and finished with 36 for the second half and a round of 75.

Moreover, as he now pointed out reasonably enough to a relieved wife, everyone is under pressure when he feels that he might win one of the great prizes. Sam King missed a little putt on the last, to finish three behind instead of two. And as the news of Cotton's troubles spread among the field behind him, so did the errors.

Ward missed a succession of chances, finishing four behind, even with the bonus of a hole-in-one at the thirteenth. Arthur Lees, like King, was at one point in his round up with Cotton, but his putting deserted him towards the end and he finished his round three behind.

The old favourite Alf Padgham gathered a big gallery around him as the news spread that he was making a charge. He went out perfectly in 34, then started back with three fours and a two. He seemed likely to tie if not lead at lunch, but at that point an excited supporter told him of Cotton's faltering ahead of him. The strokes then slipped away from Padgham over the last few holes. He finished with a 71 to be only two behind, but he was intensely conscious that it might have been much better.

Like King, he missed a very short putt on the eighteenth, and these errors affected both of them. They had to lunch on those bitter aperitifs, and neither threatened in the final stages: King had a 76 and Padgham a 77.

But before most of these dramatic happenings, we were away in the afternoon round for the last lap. After a glorious iron shot to the third, Cotton missed a short putt for a three, and I wondered if his tortures of the morning were to be repeated when he three-putted the fourth. At the ninth, he missed his only fairway of the week. It cost him a five. He was out in 37, with King still hanging on grimly with 36.

Then Cotton played four perfect holes, and I saw the serenity and confidence oozing back into him. At the fourteenth, he was off line with his second, and it cost him a five, but he put that right immediately with a five-yard putt for a three at the fifteenth. He played the sixteenth and seventeenth flawlessly in three and four, to leave himself with a four for a 71.

But the greatest drama was still to come. He drove beautifully up the middle of the eighteenth, then pushed his second into the bunker to the right of the green. When he arrived at the ball, it lay right under the precipitous face. When his first attempt left the ball there, it seemed that disaster might overtake him at the very last. You must remember that he was out at the front of the field, and it was quite impossible for anyone to compute at that stage what a winning score might be. The shots he dropped here might at the end of the day cost him the Open.

As the six-deep ranks of spectators buzzed with excitement and conjecture, Henry Cotton appeared the calmest man in that crowded scene. He studied the ball in its evil position for a few seconds, then played it beautifully out to within ten feet of the hole. Then he dusted the sand from the clothing I had laid out so carefully for him that morning, studied the line of the putt for a moment as the hush fell around him, and directed it into the heart of the hole.

I think we knew then that he had won, but there were hours of waiting before it could be confirmed. Cotton went back to the house we had taken over for the week of the championship. I remained at the course and spent much of my time in the telephone box, reporting the scores of the various hopefuls behind him as they fell by the wayside, persuading him finally that he could ex- pect to be presented with the old claret jug when he

166

returned to the clubhouse. It was a long wait, one which the modern professional, going out at the end of the field if he is in contention, does not have to endure.

In the end, he was home by five clear shots. At forty-one, struggling in the run-up to the championship with bad health and indifferent putting, he had produced what in many ways was the greatest of his triumphs. The field had not the massive American strength it had had in 1937, but he had scattered many fine players with his superb second round, then recovered magnificently when it seemed his ageing nerves might bring him down in the third. He had demonstrated his mastery throughout the week, becoming one of the very few players to win the Open after leading the qualifiers.

When it was all over, he was very tired. His face was grey with fatigue when he said to me in the privacy of the house that night, 'I'm glad we showed them I can still do it, Hargreaves. Somehow, I don't think I shall win the Open again.'

Those words came back to me as I slid into an exhausted sleep that night, bringing a sharp shaft of sadness into the contentment.

CHAPTER TWELVE

THE LONG GOODBYE

COTTON WAS RIGHT, UNFORTUNATELY. AFTER 1948 HIS GAME
and his health went into a gradual decline. The major
stomach surgery which had followed his being invalided
out of the RAF was successful, but he was never as strong
again after it. Indeed, by athletic standards, he became
frail as he moved through his forties. He was no longer
able to summon the stamina that was necessary to win
major titles – remember that the Open then involved a
gruelling marathon of six rounds in five days, with the last
two played on the same day.

Much to his dismay, he was unfit to defend his Open
Championship in 1949. He had also to inform the PGA
that he was not well enough to play in the Ryder Cup,
which was held that year at Ganton. He had been attached
since the war to the Royal Mid-Surrey Club, but in the
early fifties his friend Raymond Oppenheimer persuaded
him to move to Temple Golf Club, in Berkshire.

Oppenheimer built a fine new apartment for the Cottons, and Toots furnished it lavishly, with all of the glass and light fittings coming from Harrods. It was not quite so opulent nor so atmospheric as the Eaton Square apartment, but from its elevated position it had a magnificent view over the course towards the Thames.

The ladies' clubhouse became a fine new shop for Cotton. He equipped it almost as lavishly as the pre-war shop at Ashridge which had been destroyed by fire. The ladies were given new accommodation, on the floor beneath the Cottons' new flat. As Raymond Oppenheimer virtually owned the course, he did pretty much as he liked!

The new base gave Ivy all the facilities of a new kitchen to prepare her meals for the household. In 1949, the R & A finally gave me back my amateur status, which I had lost because of my part in the stage act of 1939! I was able to play in competitions again, when I had the time.

Our son Robert was born at Temple in 1954. From Harrods, the Cottons sent us everything a baby could possibly need. They were both very taken with the baby, and it was obvious to us then how much they had wanted a son of their own. Toots's daughters both came with her from her previous marriage in Argentina. The Cottons would have loved to adopt Robert, but there was no question of that happening.

Then Madam suggested that they would take over all the financial responsibilities of Robert's upbringing and schooling, but we politely refused, and for once she quietly accepted another point of view from her own. They were always very kind to Robert. I can see Henry in my mind's eye now, playing football for hours on end with my three-year-old son, until both of them collapsed laughing and exhausted.

And the golf which had for so many years been the passion of employer and employee went on. Cotton was still much in demand, and we journeyed about the country to meet his various commitments. The decline in his powers was minimal, but at the top level that is all that is necessary to stop winning. At first I noticed nothing more than a slight falling away of his putting, which had always been excellent in phases rather than consistently brilliant.

At Lytham in the Open of 1952, he was still good enough to come fourth, the top English finisher at forty-five. He was almost fifty when he finished sixth at Hoylake in 1956, playing now from Temple. When the Open was televised live for the first time in 1957, he stirred much excitement with his third-round 69; he played as well as that in each round, but his putting ensured that he finished only ninth, as Locke enjoyed his fourth triumph. When Peter Thomson won the first of his Opens at Lytham in 1958, the fifty-one-year-old Cotton still finished eighth, with a 68 and a 69 among his rounds.

But he found the strain of two rounds on the last day too much for him – it was not until 1966 that the championship was extended to four days. And exemptions from qualifying for the better players were still several years away. 'It's coming, but it will be too late to help me,' the old warrior said with a weary smile as we packed his clubs into the car.

He decided that there would be no more serious golf. He was spending more and more of his time abroad. The Cottons had tried to persuade Ivy and me to go with them, but we were too conservative to consider living permanently abroad, and we wanted young Robert to be brought up and educated in his own country.

Henry captained the Ryder Cup team of 1953. He took his duties very seriously; he and Toots were at Wentworth, scene of many of his former triumphs, for twelve hours a day. He was bitterly disappointed when Peter Alliss and Bernard Hunt made the putting lapses at the end of their matches which meant that the cup was not after all recaptured. Characteristically, he was most concerned of all about the repercussions upon the players involved. I know he thought that Alliss might well have been his natural successor, and attributed the putting weakness which was to be his Achilles' heel partly to that fiercely publicized lapse on the last green at Wentworth, when the Cup appeared to be there for the taking.

Cotton was instrumental in securing for me the steward's post at Temple, with Ivy employed alongside me in the way common in golf clubs. We thoroughly enjoyed the work, but it was a real wrench to leave the Cottons. Both of us missed the lively presence of Toots, who had been kindness itself to us, despite her quickness of temper with her eminent spouse. Their sparring matches were as entertaining as ever, and by this time we both knew that some at least of them were staged for the entertainment of the bemused onlookers. The affection between them grew ever deeper as they moved towards the old age that each of them secretly feared.

When the Cottons left Temple, Toots asked the Committee for a nominal hundred pounds for the sumptuous furniture and light fittings in the apartment they had occupied. It was a tremendous bargain, for they had cost over £2,000, but the request was refused. It was not a wise decision.

When it was communicated to that formidable lady, she went round the rooms with her 5-iron, which she had always thought her best club, and demolished everything in sight with a formidable vigour. From a hundred yards away, Ivy and I listened and marvelled at the energy involved. When Toots had gone and the secretary peeped fearfully into the debris that remained, there was little which could be salvaged.

Cotton had become interested now in golf course design. He decided that his most fitting memorial would be a fine course. At Penina, in Portugal, he saw the potential in what everyone else, including Toots, regarded as an unpromising area of marshland. He would create his dream course, with a luxurious clubhouse and practice facilities, and he would live there himself for the rest of his life.

The Cottons made one more attempt to persuade us to join them in their new residence. 'You need never see snow and frost again, Hargreaves!' said Henry. He remembered the bitter winter of 1947 which had driven me back to him when we froze in Derbyshire. But we were proof against all blandishments to move away from our native shore. I was by this time secretary at the rapidly expanding Downshire Municipal course, happy as always to be making my living from golf and golfers.

Henry built his course, and the world came to play on it and pay tribute to him. The course was completed in 1966. The Cottons built themselves a splendid house, Casa Branca, beside the first tee. Henry was director of golf, a sixty-year-old legend who drew a steady stream of visitors to the five-star hotel on which the course depended.

There were plenty of local servants to be trained by Toots to fulfil the functions within the house which Ivy and I had had, but I am not sure I was flattered by what Henry described as my replacement as caddie. It was the donkey Pacifico, whom he trained to carry his clubs and stand patiently whilst he instructed his clients. Henry always grew very attached to any animal he had about him, and Pacifico became a famous local character, featuring in many holiday photographs.

For some years the Cottons were happier than they had ever been. There were, inevitably, still occasions when Toots took the kind of decisive action we remembered so well. The first professional tournament at Penina was the Algarve Open. Cotton, anticipating the modern need for a course that could be flexible in length to provide for all kinds of golfers, had designed tees of great length. From the back of them, the course measured almost 7,400 yards, and that is the course he intended that the professionals should play.

One of the officials set the tees so far forward that he took some six hundred yards off the course, enabling the professionals to bring in very low scores on the fast-running ground in the first round. Cotton was furious and did not care to conceal it: to his mind, the test of a good course was whether 'the cream came to the top', and a course which was too short became a golfing lottery.

He did not succeed in convincing the officials of his case, but Toots crept out at dead of night and moved the markers for the second day to the very backs of the tees, so that there was not even room to tee up a foot behind the line of the markers in some cases. The course was played at its full length; the scores rose accordingly; the best ones came from the best players.

Neither Toots nor Henry ever publicly confessed to the manoeuvre; it was only years later that he confirmed to me a little sheepishly that she had acted with characteristic force on his behalf. I was far away in England, but I knew exactly what had happened when I read about the exchanges, because Toots, who was never slow to give her opinions, would say nothing at all. Had she been innocent, she would certainly have proclaimed the fact. She would not deny her action, for she never told a lie. To those of us who knew her well, her silence was eloquent from a thousand miles away.

In the political confusion which followed the fall of the Portuguese dictator Salazar, Cotton was accused of 'profiteering through exploitation' at Penina, and moved for a time to Sotogrande, near Gibraltar. They were not easy times, for Toots's considerable fortune had largely disappeared when the Perons took over in post-war Argentina; but the owner knocked two apartments into one and the Cottons settled in to live as comfortably as ever. Even Pacifico was smuggled across the border to join them, dying exhausted but happy among a harem of fillies which had been assembled for polo.

Then Henry had a nasty fall on a stone staircase. Toots must have been anxious about him, for when he did not respond to treatment she conquered her lifetime fear of flying, chartered a private 'air ambulance', and flew with him to the King George V Hospital in Paris. It turned out that he had three broken ribs, a ruptured spleen, and a punctured lung. The pneumonia which so often follows upon shock had set in. He had three major operations, and hung for a week and more between life and death.

His illness was the prelude to a bizarre happening for

174

me. I was by this time manager at Puttenham Golf Club, near Guildford, very busy with the work of a rapidly expanding club. One night I had a phone call from Toots's daughter Chickie, whom I had known since she was a child. 'It's about Henry,' she said, knowing, I suppose, that that would secure from me whatever service I could offer. She had called her stepfather 'Henry' ever since she was three years old.

'I wonder if you can do me a favour, Ernest. Henry's in a coma in hospital in Paris. Even Mum can't bring him out of it. All his friends have been to see him, but none of them can get through to him. It's a long shot, but we're desperate. Mum thinks a voice he knew for so many years might just work. Do you think you could try ringing him, just on the off-chance?'

I agreed, of course, and she gave me the number. Being brought up in the era before telephones entered general use, I have never been particularly happy with them, and I have no doubt I sounded nervous and diffident when I asked for the Matron and tried to explain my strange commission.

She had already been prepared for the attempt, and needed no explanation. She must have been sitting beside the patient's bed when I rang, for she said immediately, 'I'll put the phone to Mr Cotton's ear: just speak slowly and clearly.'

The line was very good, better than we often got on a local call to the next village. I could hear the faint rasp of shallow breathing. Feeling anxious and rather foolish, I said only, 'Mr Cotton?'

There was scarcely a pause before a familiar voice, weak but surprisingly clear, said simply, 'Hargreaves.' In that moment I was glad as never before that we had never

175

departed from our unvarying forms of address as master and servant.

Henry recovered consciousness, and a delighted Toots rang me the next day to thank me for my efforts, as effusive as if I had been an eminent surgeon. I cannot explain the event: I think I was more surprised than anyone that he should come out of his coma like that. We have more and more evidence as we move towards the end of the century that the human mind is a strange and unpredictable thing. I have always presumed that Henry must have been ready to surface from his coma, and that I was merely the lifebelt which was thrown to him at the right moment.

At any rate, he made a full recovery. Toots persuaded him that the best therapy would be golf, and prevailed upon him to accept the invitation of the Royal and Ancient to play in the 1977 Open at Turnberry, to mark the fiftieth anniversary of his first appearance in the championship. She was right, in that the commitment gave him the incentive to get as fit as possible and work hard on his game. I went with him to Turnberry, with Madam's brisk instruction to watch over him ringing in my ears.

He had made a good recovery, but at seventy he looked to me distressingly frail. He was playing with Arnold Palmer, the most charismatic golfer of his era, and Christie O'Connor, the darling of the Irish and perhaps their greatest ever player. Both of them were then past their best but still actively competing on the golfing circuits.

The illustrious trio drew a huge gallery, before which poor Henry scored 93. It did not really matter: no-one expected a man of seventy who had nearly died a few months earlier to do better – except Henry, who had wanted to show the world that he could still play a bit.

He hit the ball almost as straight as ever, though he had inevitably lost length. What he had not been able to prepare for was the pace of play, which would not have been tolerated in his era and should not be in ours. He had always prepared himself meticulously for each shot, and had been criticized by players like George Duncan for being too slow. But he had expected to get round in tournament play in three hours, and was apologetic on the occasions when the huge, unroped crowds which followed him had led to his taking three and a quarter.

Now it took almost five hours for us to get round. It was beyond not just his physical but his mental capacity, and his concentration deserted him over the closing holes. I suffered more in that round than I have ever done on a golf course. Every poor shot drove a shaft into me, reviving sharp, contrasting memories of the great days which were gone for ever.

After that, Henry played no more in public. He continued to dispense sound and free advice to young professionals, as he had done to the young Tony Jacklin, who we thought for some years would replace him, but who had a sadly short time at the top. Of those who qualified for the last two rounds as the exhausted Cotton stole away from Turnberry, the one who finished last was a certain N. A. Faldo; he went to the old master for tuition in the next year and has not done too badly for himself since then.

Cotton enjoyed radio and early television commentating with his old friend Henry Longhurst, and he continued to write books and articles on the game he loved. To the last, he exhorted anyone who would listen to take up his 'tyre drill', hitting an old car tyre for several minutes daily to build up the strength of the hands, the key to good golf shots.

I last saw him in action at Tewkesbury Park, where I spent the last twelve years of my golfing life as starter, before retiring at the age of seventy-nine. He was staying with his old friend Sir William Carr, and he came down to see me and give a few lessons. He brought a tyre with him and insisted on well-bred ladies attacking it as hard as they could, exhorting them to greater efforts as though it were a live thing, like an old-fashioned sergeant urging on his men to bloodthirsty bayonet drill.

On Christmas Eve 1982, he and Toots played nine holes of golf together at Penina and then attended evening Mass. On the morning of Christmas Day, after they had exchanged presents, she died suddenly and quietly. She was a little older than her husband; in her own unique manner, she had supported and organized her Henry for almost fifty years.

I don't think he ever recovered properly from her death. I saw him once more, when he was the subject of the television programme *This Is Your Life* in 1986, and I appeared with many of his old friends before the cameras. It was sad to see him at the party afterwards without his beloved Toots. He was glad to see us and talk over the old times, but he had the air of a man waiting for death. For one of his serene faith, that was not illogical; he was merely anxious to rejoin his beloved wife. If they are together somewhere now, it will be a noisier and a livelier place for their presence.

For Henry had only a few years to wait till his own death. Unfortunately this was long enough to see his dream course at Penina reshaped and distorted.

Eventually the folly of this was realized and the reforms were reversed. But the owners' change of heart came too late for Cotton, who was dead by then. He had left Penina in despair, living out his last months with Chickie in London.

He died before he could receive the knighthood which was so long overdue; Buckingham Palace announced that he should be known posthumously as Sir Henry Cotton. On Boxing Day 1987, he was buried alongside Toots, a little way from his beloved Penina.

I am an old man myself now, and I had not been in regular touch with him for some time when he died. But my own life still feels diminished by his passing.

CHAPTER THIRTEEN

MY FAVOURITE GOLFERS

I HAVE NOW BEEN WATCHING GOLF FOR SEVENTY YEARS. FOR almost sixty of them, I was actively involved in the game. What follows is derived from my observations. It is in no sense an attempt to put great golfers in an order of precedence, which is a fascinating but ultimately futile exercise. Bob Jones's verdict on Nicklaus, 'He plays a game with which I am not familiar', is the most gracious of compliments on the younger man's awesome powers. But it is not a definitive judgement: it says as much about Jones's generosity of spirit as it does about Nicklaus's skills.

Nor have I endeavoured to be comprehensive: the omission of both Ben Hogan and Jack Nicklaus is sufficient proof of that. The golfers who follow are those whom I got to know as men and whose play I loved to watch. I think all of them are great players, but they represent an individual preference.

180

Harry Vardon

I saw all three of the 'great triumvirate' play, but Vardon fascinated me more than Taylor or Braid. He was well past his best when I first saw him as a boy, though he continued to play the regular exhibition matches which the best golfers of his era relied upon to support themselves.

As a star-struck youngster, I watched Taylor and Braid avidly, but it was Vardon who left the indelible impression. The other two attacked the ball with a fierceness which reminded one that these players had all begun in the days of the gutty ball. Taylor lashed at the ball with a flat swing from a flat-footed stance, his effort echoed in the little grunt which accompanied every full shot. Horace Hutchinson summarized Braid when he spoke of the 'divine fury' which was the hallmark of his striking. He settled over the ball with a portentous gravity; the sudden furious lash he then aimed at it came as a perpetual surprise after these deliberate preparations. Bernard Darwin, who had lived and played through the great age of the gutty, said that he never saw anyone hit so malignantly hard at the ball.

Vardon in contrast was all grace and ease. He had an upright swing, and he hit the ball very high, but what made me gasp when I first saw him was the astonishing ease with which he hit the ball great distances. You may notice that he is the only one of the three whom I think of as *swinging*: the other two *hit* at the ball in an older method.

Vardon was in many senses a pioneer. He established the idea that the golfer should swing at the ball, relying on perfect rhythm and timing for his distance and accuracy. These things are now accepted as truisms, but in Vardon's

181

day they were almost revolutionary. He did not invent the grip which bears his name, but he popularized it and explained to millions how it worked. Memory plays tricks, but I still think of Vardon as the most graceful and rhythmic swinger of a golf club I ever saw.

He had to be, for his hickory shafts were very light: we caddies compared notes eagerly on these things in the days when clubs varied so much more than today. He rarely carried more than seven or eight clubs, and never more then ten, however important the occasion – another habit which might be expected to endear him to caddies!

Vardon was also the model professional. Like Jack Hobbs at cricket, he dignified his profession, and was much more of a gentleman than some who called themselves such. He was a great thinker about the game he loved, and most generous in his advice to those who followed him. Henry Cotton learned much during his trips to North and South America, but he always maintained that he learned even more from Vardon.

Cotton described Vardon as the purest striker of a golf ball he ever saw, hitting the ball early *with the clubhead* and taking very little turf with his irons. Vardon always thought his greatest triumph was his Open of 1903: it was certainly the most remarkable in the history of the old championship. He came to play in it against doctor's orders, feared that he would never be able to complete his last round, though he entered upon it with a lead of seven strokes, and was ordered to a sanatorium for several months after his success.

Harry Vardon won the first of his six British Opens almost a century ago and the US Open as long ago as 1900; but in the techniques he developed he was the first modern golfer.

Bob Jones

He is almost universally known as Bobby, but here at least I have given him the first name he always preferred for himself.

There is a link between the golfers who are my first two choices, and I found a sentence of Bernard Darwin's which expresses it perfectly: 'Harry Vardon and Bobby Jones combined exquisiteness of art with utterly relentless precision in a way not quite given to any other golfers.'

I was fortunate that my first Open Championship, at Royal Lytham in 1926, coincided with Jones's first title; he won by two strokes. Next year, at St Andrews, where he had once picked up his ball in despair, he won by six shots, and the supposedly dour Scots crowd rushed on to the Tom Morris green to lift the 'invader' shoulder high in spontaneous and generous tribute. At Hoylake in 1930 he won his third Open, completing 'the impregnable quadrilateral' of the Open and Amateur championships of Britain and the USA in the same year. Then he retired, at the ripe old age of twenty-eight.

But I have not chosen him merely because of the brilliant and brief supremacy he achieved. Like the others in my selection, he made you feel wonderfully close to him as he played his golf. He was no cold machine, but suffered on the course as did other and lesser mortals. His behaviour in Britain was impeccable, though we were told that in his youth he had been given to throwing his clubs about. In an era when the predominance of match-play made these things more apparent, he was always the most sporting and gracious of opponents.

His trials came with his own game, as he sought the perfection which must always ultimately elude even the best. He could rarely eat anything before he played, and he was

183

reputed to lose up to a stone during the stress of the great championships. On occasions he broke into tears, not through distress but through sheer emotional overstrain.

If you saw the state in which he finished a round, you appreciated the courage which it took for Jones to fight as he did with his own temperament upon the course and to accept disasters so gracefully. He bore the cruel illness which deposited him in a wheelchair in later life with the same smiling, unflinching fortitude.

I have said that he was a graceful stylist, like Vardon. He relied, like the man born thirty-two years before him, on rhythm and timing. Because he was perfectly balanced, he stood with his feet very close together – so close that Walter Hagen found the stance impossible when he experimented with imitations of it. Watching him closely, I decided that he did not swing quite as slowly as Vardon; it was rather that he *appeared* to swing slowly, almost lazily, because everything in the swing was so perfectly balanced and co-ordinated.

Jones won everything he set out to achieve, mostly by vast margins. Then he retired gracefully from the fray, to pursue his other interests and emphasize what is nowadays too often forgotten: at the end of the day, golf is only a game.

Walter Hagen

I suppose you would expect me to choose my old master, the man who first encouraged me to think that I might make a living from the game I loved. But there is more than sentiment in the choice.

Hagen was a pioneer in almost every sense. As early as 1919, he became the first tournament professional, after his second US Open victory, dispensing with the usual practice of having a club attachment. He also took golfers out of Norfolk jackets and breeches and into bright woollen cardigans and two-tone shoes.

But these were superficial things. It was Hagen and Cotton who transformed the world of professional golf as it was when I came to it in the twenties. Hagen had begun, like most American professionals of his day, as a caddie. He recognized no social barriers, and in America his skill and his charisma ensured that few were put in his way. But when he came to Britain he found that professionals were not even allowed into the clubhouse.

He did not just hire a Rolls-Royce, but a butler as well, to serve him caviar, smoked salmon and champagne in the car park whilst the members watched glumly from inside their clubhouses. When he thought professionals were treated as second-class citizens at a famous Scottish course, he refused to go in to be presented with his prize, but took his caddie and spectators off for a drink in the hotel where he was staying. And how could I omit a man who won the Open and then presented me, his caddie, with his entire prize money? Walter had style.

And he carried that style on to the course with him. I have never seen anyone so relaxed when playing in major championships. He chatted happily to spectators between strokes and laughed at his bad ones, a habit I should like to see some modern players cultivate. He never refused an autograph, even on the course, though it is fair to say that spectators as well as players were more disciplined in his day, and no-one dreamed of asking him for one while he was playing serious golf.

He played plenty of bad shots: more than I have seen any other major player perpetrate. During exhibition matches I am sure he sometimes played indifferent strokes on purpose, or at least played carelessly, so that he could demonstrate the virtuosity of his recovery play. This was the greatest I have ever seen (the nearest modern equivalent to him in this would be Ballesteros, but I have not often watched the Spanish wizard at close quarters), and it was the key to Hagen's game. He was the finest improviser of golf shots I ever saw – he could 'ad-lib' a shot, as we caddies used to call it, for any situation. He used hickory shafts throughout his greatest days, and he had a better feel for the 'whip' of hickory into the ball, a finer touch on the ball, than anyone else I saw.

Of all the great golfers, he was at first sight the least impressive. He had a wide stance, like many of the older players, and he swayed a lot on every shot: at times it became a lurch. He was the most debonair of golfers in dress and bearing, but he never had a pretty swing. His head did not lift, but it moved a considerable amount backwards and forwards on every stroke. But he had the finest cohesion of hand and brain that I ever saw.

He was the first golfer to demonstrate to me the importance of temperament in winning championships. Percy Boomer wrote of him in 1946:

> *Nothing*, neither wind nor weather, bad greens, tight corners, nor unduly chatty opponents, ever made the Haig *tense* . . . I remember talking to him at Sandwich on the day he won the British Open. He had finished and we sat and chatted for a long time while waiting to see if George Duncan would deprive him of the title which otherwise he had won. Well, George very nearly did it, but Walter Hagen never batted an

eyelid. He was as chatty, as cheerful, and as untense as ever – at the end of a week's competitive golf with the whole issue of a three thousand mile trip in the balance.

I saw that unflappable temperament take him round Muirfield in the gales of 1929, producing twice in one day exactly the scores he had forecast would be necessary, when you would have sworn that the wind made rational calculations impossible.

Other men played better, quite often. But no man was so secure with himself on a golf course: the bigger the occasion, the cooler was the Haig. That was the man who helped me to grow up. The man who travelled the world to play, and charmed all about him, even as he took their money and their titles.

The man who loved to play, but loved the life which golf brought to him even more.

Gene Sarazen
Gene was born Eugene Saraceni, and when he came to Moortown to play in the Ryder Cup of 1929 it seemed that every Italian ice-cream seller in Yorkshire had turned out to support him. He had changed his name mainly because of the prejudice against Italian immigrants in some parts of America, and also because he said it made him sound like a violinist rather than a sportsman!

I was a boy of sixteen when I first met him at Moortown, and I identified immediately with him. He was not much taller than I was, and with his boyish good looks and his unassuming manner he seemed only a little older – he was in fact twenty-seven. While I was waiting to caddie for Hagen, he chatted to me as though I was an equal. 'I'm just a caddie myself, who's learned to play a little golf,' he said.

He had begun life as a carpenter, turning to caddying to get out into the open air for the sake of his health. He showed me some of the wood-shaping craftsmanship he had exercised upon his own hickory-shafted clubs, in those days at Moortown when I walked in the company of the world's great golfers as though in a dream.

He was one of the game's natural golfers, never having to work at his golf as Cotton and others did. The game came to him so quickly that he won the US Open and the PGA at the age of twenty. A year later he made the long trip across the Atlantic to compete in the British Open at Troon, failed to qualify, and broke down in his humiliation. To his eternal credit, he resolved to come back until he won. After several near-misses, he won gloriously by a clear five shots at Sandwich in 1932.

He was the first man to win all four of the modern 'majors'. He invented the sand wedge, and ensured that for the great golfers bunkers would never again hold the terrors they had in the past.

But these are my favourite golfers among the many I knew, and it needs more than a secure place in the history of the game to get them into my personal gallery. I have hinted at the charm and friendliness of the little olive-skinned man, but there is more to it than that.

Sarazen was the most attacking golfer I ever saw in the first half of the century – I have to make that qualification, for there is another in my gallery with a claim to the description. In those days when the equipment available meant that even the big hitters were thirty yards or so short of their modern equivalents with the wooden clubs, Gene went for everything. Bob Jones said of him,

'It was bang! bang! bang! all the time . . . he has been forever the impatient, headstrong player who went for everything.'

That approach lost him a few titles, but it won him far more. And it produced from him one of the most famous shots in golf. As he came towards the end of his last round in the Masters in 1935, his caddie counselled that he should lay up safely short on the par five fifteenth. But Gene went for the green with his 4-wood, and holed the shot for an albatross two. It took him into a play-off, which he won to complete his 'set' of great titles. That one stroke, which he told me years later was worth more to him financially than any of his championships, also established the infant Masters in the public mind as a great tournament. Fittingly, Sarazen was still opening the Masters with an exhibition nine holes at the age of ninety, disgusted with the quality of his golf but as cheerful as ever.

In his second US Open win, in 1932, Sarazen played his last twenty-eight holes in 100 strokes, including a final round of 66. It was a feat which Jones called 'the finest competitive exhibition on record'.

Gene Sarazen had a small man's compactness and control in his swing. He was entirely self-taught – indeed the only problems he ever had came when for a period in the late twenties he became obsessed with theory. He had a simple, straightforward swing, sturdy and muscular throughout, but utterly without frills: the swing which I always thought every amateur of his build should imitate.

Bernard Darwin said that it was impossible to think of Sarazen without his smile, because that was the outward and visible sign of his personality and his golf. In 1973, at the age of seventy-one, he came for one last time to

189

compete in the Open at Troon, the scene of his humiliation fifty years earlier. I had not seen him for over twenty years, but he recognized me immediately and chatted as if we had met the previous week.

Cotton was not playing, so I followed the little man for one last time. On the postage-stamp eighth, where once he would have played a 9-iron, he decided he needed to punch in a little 5-iron. Before millions of television viewers around the world, the ball bounced gently up to the hole and dropped in for a hole in one.

Bernard Darwin had been dead then for twelve years. But he would have been delighted to see the broad smile which he saw as Gene's trade-mark lighting up the course.

Tony Lema

Why have I put among my favourites a man I saw only twice, and that for no more than a week at a time?

There are three reasons: the towering stature of his achievement in the first of those weeks; the immediate warmth of his personality; and the sheer beauty of his swing and his golf.

Lema was a caddie at twelve and a marine in the Korean War. Perhaps because of these beginnings, he had an immediate rapport with those of us who earned our livings on the humbler fringes of golf. In a game which has come to take itself too seriously, he was the nearest modern equivalent I have found to Walter Hagen.

It was not just that 'Champagne Tony' had a well-publicized liking for the good things of life. He gave, as the Haig had, the impression of a man simply enjoying himself. Like Hagen also, he concealed beneath his debonair exterior a steely determination to win the big prizes and a confidence in his own ability.

190

In July 1964, having won three major American tournaments within a few weeks, he came to St Andrews for the British Open. This is the venue which had reduced the immortal Bob Jones to picking up his ball on his first acquaintance with it, the course which more than any other demands time for the golfer to fathom its intricacies.

Lema gave himself just thirty-six hours. He played it once, and then in the evening spent hours with us in the pub, exchanging notes about the course with the caddies who had known it for years. Then he hired one of the best of them, and set out to win the Open. I waited to see such presumption brought low, and was amazed by what followed.

On the first day, gale-force winds blew in from the west, and we looked to see our new friend's game disintegrate. Instead, he drove so straight through the wind that I was reminded of Cotton at his best: there can be no higher compliment. He had a fine 73 and lay two shots off the lead. On the second day, he showed an amazing mastery of those little running shots into the green which are not needed in America, and putted magnificently on those greens which newcomers often find impossible. His 68 was the best of the day by two strokes, and he led the championship: our friend, who popped in to celebrate with us that night, might yet achieve the impossible.

On the final day, he realized that Jack Nicklaus was mounting an inspired charge as they passed each other on one of St Andrews' dual greens during the morning round. Nicklaus finished with 66 and 68, but Lema was unflappable. The tempo of his swing altered not a jot all day, he seemed at peace with himself and the world, and he won by a clear five shots.

191

Lema was killed in a plane crash two years later, and he was mourned nowhere more than in Scotland. They know their golf there, and there has been no more impressive display of talent than Lema's at St Andrews in 1964. But he won friends as well as respect that week, for he so patently enjoyed his golf and his life, and was so accessible to all around him.

In those respects, he reminded me of my first golfing master, Walter Hagen. But if you wanted poetry as well as humour in your golf, you would have chosen to watch Lema. He was a tall, handsome figure, and he had a swing to match. All those years ago when I was a boy, I learned from Harry Vardon that rhythm and balance are the secrets of the modern golf swing. Lema had those in abundance, and he added a grace and a beauty that made his swing the envy of all who saw it.

Tony Lema gave both aesthetic satisfaction and a lot of fun. It is a rare combination, which ensures him a place in my exclusive gallery.

Arnold Palmer

You probably guessed at this choice when I said that Sarazen was the most attacking golfer *in the first half of the century*. None of the golfers who have played since the Second World War has attacked the great courses more unremittingly than Palmer. That is the main reason why the public loves him, why even in his sixties 'Arnie's Army' follows him in its thousands, even when they know he will no longer win.

Nobody since Hagen has had Palmer's appeal, and no-one has ever had such a following. It is true that his career coincided with the golfing boom of the late fifties and sixties, but it was Palmer more than any single golfer who fostered that boom. He grew up steeped in golf, and he has never lost his affection for the game which has made him a multi-millionaire.

His father, who had worked in the steel mills of Pennsylvania before he became a golfing professional, passed on his humour and his strength to the son who remained so close to him. More importantly, he taught him always to remind himself how lucky he was to be making a living from golf, and always to respect the traditions of the game.

Palmer's only teacher was his father, and he has remained his own man throughout his success. He has an orthodox grip and huge hands, which are the basis of his game. I have never seen anyone hit the ball so hard and so successfully out of thick rough as Palmer. 'If you can see it you can hit it. And if you can hit it, you can hole it!' he would say. For me, that summed up his philosophy of the game more effectively than any other of his many famous sayings.

The Palmer image was established in 1960, when he won both the Masters and the US Open from positions which seemed hopeless. At Augusta he finished with three successive birdies, to beat Ken Venturi by a stroke. At the US Open at Cherry Hills, he was seven strokes behind as he went into the last round; he played the opening nine in an astonishing 30 on his way to a 65 and victory by two strokes.

And to cement his place in my affections, Palmer, at the height of his fame, came to revive American interest in the British Open. For a few years the top Americans had been patchy in their attendance at the old championship; but once Palmer had reiterated that no golfer could count himself among the élite without winning the oldest of the great titles, the best in the world know that they must come to the Open.

At the centenary Open in 1960 at St Andrews, Palmer came second by a stroke to Kel Nagle. He came back and won at Royal Birkdale in 1961, pitting his strength eagerly against the worst of the gale on the second day. In a raging wind, he played the first six holes in an unbelievable three under par: he still regards that hour as his finest, for he loved to meet the challenge of the elements.

At Troon in 1962 the challenge was very different, with the course hard and baked, and the ball running fast and not always predictably. Palmer said after he had practised that he had never played an important championship before in conditions like that, where his strength would be of little use to him. He won in a record 276, six strokes ahead of Nagle in second place and thirteen ahead of the rest!

His failures could be equally spectacular, as when he dropped seven shots to par in the 1966 US Open when he was so far in front that he set out to beat Ben Hogan's record score for the championship. But he was never afraid of failure, never made excuses, and never grudged an opponent his success.

The rewards in golf have never been greater than in the modern era, and the pressures of fame and fortune on the personalities of the winners have sometimes found them wanting. But Palmer has kept both his feet on the ground and never lost touch with the golfing enthusiasts who support him. He and his charming wife Winnie treated me as if I were a fellow golfing star, not a humble extra making up the numbers, and spent hours playing with my son Robert.

The last time I saw Palmer was when I was getting off a

late-night train in London after travelling south. It was late, he was now a veteran, and I knew he was tired after four not too successful rounds in the Open. He would not want to be bothered with small talk at that hour, I was sure. I turned away to make my way home.

'Hi, Ernest!' said a familiar voice. 'How's things with you?' At the end of a week when everyone wanted to shake his hand, he sought me out, asked about Ivy and Robert, and chatted for five minutes.

The only thing which ever separated Arnold Palmer from ordinary people was an outsize talent. Fortunately he has the heart to go with it.

Henry Cotton

Many of these pages have been concerned with the man's triumphs, so I shall not repeat myself by recalling them.

But I must say why he is one of my favourite golfers, and there is not one single reason but a collection of them. Like Hagen, Cotton was determined to live like a millionaire, whether or not he could be one. Without that determination on his part, I could never have had the life I have so enjoyed.

Cotton was in some respects the nearest British parallel to Hagen, and in others his exact opposite. In his dress and in the way he loved to live off the course, he learned from and in some ways surpassed Hagen: mere imitation was never Henry's way. His love of fine wines and fine living, his contempt for the social barriers with which lesser men sought to isolate him, were wholly akin to Hagen's.

It is to Hagen and to Cotton that the tournament professionals of today should breathe silent thanks as they

195

pick up their cheques. Others have consolidated their position in the last thirty years, but it was Hagen in America and Cotton in Britain who laid out the trails.

Yet on the course, it would be difficult to find anyone more different from Hagen than Cotton. Where Hagen loved to talk and – much rarer – loved to listen, Cotton demanded silence from those around him. The cocoon of concentration which his game demanded could admit no interference from outside. He gave everything to the shot he was playing, and to do that he had to shut out of his mind all other considerations, not just while he was playing it but during his preparations. Hagen, like Trevino after him, could switch his concentration swiftly on and off, so that he gave the maximum effort to a stroke when he had been conversing about something else only a moment earlier. Cotton knew he could never do that.

There was a corresponding difference in the golf of the two men. Hagen was an instinctive shotmaker, improvising as he saw fit for the conditions and the terrain. He was as likely to play a 150-yard shot with a 4-iron as a 7-iron; the choice was what allowed him to master British links as thoroughly as the very different inland courses in America.

Cotton on the other hand was the first of the modern breed of professionals, labouring long and hard to build up a 'grooved' swing which would serve him well for all shots. He could shape shots when he had to, as any professional must, but for preference he would always elect for the standard shot. He built his game on driving that was not only as long as anything his rivals could produce, but also much straighter, so that he could play orthodox shots into the greens from the fairways. He would have thought that the modern pros, able to hit 3-woods and 1-irons from the tee, were getting it far too easy.

But he would not have denied them the chance. He never turned down a request for help from a fellow-professional, however humble. He never failed to answer a golfing letter, and there were many thousands over the years. He was never pompous, and anyone who held a golf club had an immediate bond with him. He had a dry sense of humour and a wonderful sense of the ridiculous which the public were rarely allowed to see.

Like Jones, he had the capacity to make you suffer with him on the course, however calm his outward demeanour. Because I knew the fierce strength of his aspirations, the savage demands he made upon himself, I felt almost as drained as he was at the conclusion of each of his great achievements.

But the greatest thing about Henry Cotton was his love of the game. Even his detractors allowed him that, and those of us who loved him found it his most endearing as well as his most enduring quality. Read any one of his books to catch it. He wrote them himself, unlike most golfers. Long after he had finished playing, when many would have said he had nothing left to learn, he was still analysing not just the swings but every section of the swings of his contemporaries and those who came up behind him, trying to discover the elusive secrets of the game he loved.

I stood beside him on stage and watched him perform an act that was wildly successful, despite all the odds, not because of his humour (which for once came through) but because of his sheer love of the game and his wish to communicate its joys to others. I watched him when he

197

was old and failing, exhorting all who would listen to strengthen their hands by smashing a club into an old tyre, and leaping forward himself to demonstrate when they were not vigorous enough for him.

He called his last book *Thanks for the Game*. There never was a more appropriate title. Thanks, Henry.